THE SMARTEST
SALES BOOK
YOU'LL EVER READ

Also by Daniel R. Solin

Does Your Broker Owe You Money?

The Smartest Investment Book You'll Ever Read

The Smartest 401(k) Book You'll Ever Read

The Smartest Retirement Book You'll Ever Read

The Smartest Portfolio You'll Ever Own

The Smartest Money Book You'll Ever Read

Timeless Investment Advice

7 Steps to Save Your Financial Life Now

For bulk orders, please go to: www.danielsolin.com

For press and speaking inquiries, please contact:

Veronica Skelton
The Concept Agency
75 Broadway, Suite 202
San Francisco, CA 94111
415.342.3435
veronica@conceptagency.com

THE SMARTEST SALES BOOK YOU'LL EVER READ

The Truth About Successful Selling

Daniel R. Solin

New York Times bestselling author of the
Smartest series of books

THE SMARTEST SALES BOOK YOU'LL EVER READ
Copyright © Daniel R. Solin, 2014
Silvercloud Publishing, LLC
Bonita Springs, FL 34134

ISBN 978-0-9860478-0-0

Library of Congress Control Number:
LCCN 2013914952
Printed in Canada

Solin, Daniel R.
  The smartest sales book you'll ever read : the truth about successful selling /
Daniel R. Solin.

     p. ; cm. -- (Smartest series)

  Issued also as ePub, ePDF and mobi ebooks.
  Includes bibliographical references and index.
  ePub ISBN: 0-9748763-0-5
  ePDF ISBN: 0-9748763-1-3
  mobi ISBN: 0-9748763-2-1
  ISBN: 978-0-9860478-0-0

  1. Selling. 2. Success in business. I. Title.

HF5438.25 .S65 2013
658.85   2013914952

To Mandy, Margarette, Paula, and Theresa
Women with true grit

CONTENTS

INTRODUCTION

Happy cows give more milk,
and happy salespeople tend to sell more.
—Wendy Connick

There's a much better way to close sales and find happiness than walking on hot coals and repeating mantras. I didn't know that for certain until I did the research for this book.

My intention initially was to focus entirely on the research showing how you could increase your sales. This is a subject that has fascinated me for a long time. Over my career as a lawyer, investment advisor, and author, I have "sold" hundreds of millions of dollars of legal and financial advisory services and hundreds of thousands of books. There are few mistakes I have *not* made. One stands out: I talked too much and listened too little. I placed a premium on *conveying* information and didn't understand that the key to success was the ability to *obtain* it.

I was highly motivated to be financially successful. I attended courses and read everything I could find about effective salesmanship, but most of the "sales advice" made me uncomfortable. It seemed formulaic and manipulative. The people teaching these courses were everything I thought successful people should be: affable, outgoing, charming, and charismatic. I am not. The thought of going into a room where I know no one and having to introduce myself still ranks as one of my least favorite activities. I can't imagine "overcoming sales obstacles" with standard phrases. I was struck by the underlying assumption, which no one (including me) ever challenged: "Stay focused on increasing sales. That's the only goal that matters."

Here's where I was led in a different direction. I thought increased sales meant more income, and more income meant a higher level of happiness. I was wrong. I had it backwards. Making more money (after you reach a baseline level of income) is unlikely to make you happier. But being happier is likely to make you more successful. I was missing the "happiness forest" for the "income trees."

This discovery led me to expand the scope of the book. Instead of just discussing how to close more sales (which I do in Parts One and Two), I also present ways you can become happier (Part Three). Fortunately, there's an overlap between core skills that will increase your income and activities that will make you happier.

There's a lot of misinformation in books dealing with sales and self-help topics. (It's interesting that rarely are these two subjects discussed in the same book.) Quick fixes are appealing because they don't take much time or effort. They also aren't very effective, as you'll see. Since it's just as important to understand what doesn't work as what does, I debunk some of the common myths about success and happiness in Chapter 1.

This book follows the same successful format as my *Smartest* series of investment books. It's straightforward, clear, and concise. I don't expect you to rely solely on my views. All of my recommendations are supported by studies and articles, referenced in the notes section (which is entitled "Need More Convincing?"). I summarize the main idea of each chapter in a text box called "What's the Point?"

I hope you find within these pages the keys to living a happier, more prosperous, and more fulfilling life.

PART ONE

Traits Of
Successful Salespeople

CHAPTER 1

Pragmatism

It is the laws of physics that protect your feet,
not the ramblings of a self-help guru.
—Steven Novella, MD

Successful salespeople are pragmatists. They are realistic about their own abilities. They focus their efforts on activities that are actually likely to increase their sales. Hokey, quick-fix programs don't distract them. Popular efforts to increase success by "feeling good about yourself" fall squarely within the category of a distraction. In fact, pursuing those tactics can convert "self-help" into self-delusion and narcissism.

Self-Help Is Big Business

By some estimates, the self-improvement market is a $9.6 billion industry. You can seek to solve your issues by studying books, videos, audio programs, and infomercials; attending seminars, workshops, and holistic institutes; and hiring personal coaches. Leading motivational speakers have become household names and enormously successful. They include Tony Robbins, Deepak Chopra, Phil McGraw, "Dr. Laura," Brian Tracy, the late Zig Ziglar, and many others.

Unfortunately, many of the most popular self-help books are based solely on the views of the author, without reference to any data. Steven Novella, an academic clinical neurologist at the Yale University School of Medicine, correctly observed that despite the ready availability of a vast amount of research dealing with the subjects discussed in self-help books, the big sellers "seem to be completely disconnected from that evidence. What they are selling are made-up easy answers, personality, and gimmicks." The "common hook" of these books, Novella notes, is the flawed view that you can materially improve your life by just thinking about better outcomes. Much of the advice in these catch phrase–laden books is demonstrably wrong, but both the message and the messengers are very appealing if you are looking for an easy solution to complex problems.

Feel-Good Concepts: Self-Esteem and Self-Confidence

Many self-help books and programs hinge on the idea that success depends on boosting your self-esteem and self-confidence. Proponents of this idea often use the two terms interchangeably. However, self-esteem and self-confidence are not the same thing.

According to psychotherapist Emily Roberts, "self-esteem" refers to overall feelings about your self-worth. Someone with low self-esteem may feel inadequate, helpless, and a victim of other people or events. "Self-confidence" refers to how you perceive your ability to handle a particular situation. I may feel generally good about my overall life, but lack confidence when speaking to large groups. If so, I would have good self-esteem, but low self-confidence in that situation.

It's easier to improve your self-confidence than your self-esteem. For example, if you lack confidence in your public speaking skills, you could take courses in public speaking and practice before family and friends as a way to boost your confidence.

Boosting self-esteem is more challenging, for reasons I'll explain later. But that hasn't stopped dozens of gurus from claiming they can teach you easy "feel-good" fixes that will change your life.

The Premise of Self-Help Gurus

Proponents of boosting self-esteem and self-confidence often advocate doing so through "positive thinking." For example, author and motivational speaker Brian Tracy believes self-esteem is the "reactor core" of your personality. He notes that "developing and maintaining high levels of self-esteem is the most important thing you can do, every day, in building yourself to the point where you are capable of achieving all your goals." How do you achieve this good opinion of yourself? Tracy counsels focusing on your successes and repeating the words "I like myself! I like myself!" again and again throughout the day. According to Tracy, these powerful words make you "feel happier and perform better."

There's a long history of psychologists and others encouraging us to repeat positive phrases like "I can do it" or "I am an attractive person." Émile Coué, a French psychologist and pharmacist in the early twentieth century, recommended repeating "Every day, in every way, I'm getting better and better."

How Good Should You Feel About Yourself?

Is feeling good about yourself a worthwhile goal? Will raising your self-esteem lead to success? There is strong evidence to the contrary.

Low self-confidence leads to success. Tomas Chamorro-Premuzic, PhD, is a leading authority on personality profiling and psychometric testing. He is a prolific author of six books and over one hundred scientific papers. His views, if generally accepted, would be a body blow to much of the lucrative self-help industry. In a blog post published on the website of the prestigious *Harvard Business Review*, Chamorro-Premuzic asserts that people with *low* self-confidence (but not extremely low) are likely to be more successful.

Why? For one thing, low self-confidence makes you more aware of your shortcomings. That ability to be self-critical can propel you to achieve success. If you are brimming with self-confidence (which appears to be the goal of many self-help gurus), you tend to ignore negative feedback.

Low self-confidence can also make you work harder to achieve your goals. You're more motivated to put in the time and effort to improve. In contrast, those who are highly confident may think that working hard to overcome limitations is for "ordinary" people. They don't put in the effort needed for success.

High self-confidence has drawbacks. According to Chamorro-Premuzic, people who are completely lacking self-doubt can easily come across as arrogant. They are less likely to admit their errors and more likely to blame others for their mistakes. In addition, there is something about supremely confident people that comes across as delusional. None of us is that wonderful. The world is a complex place, filled with shades of gray. We are all wrong sometimes in our judgments and perceptions. Chamorro-Premuzic's conclusion is blunt: "High self-confidence isn't a blessing, and low self-confidence is not a curse—in fact, it is the other way around."

Another exhaustive study supports these views. The authors concluded that preoccupation with self-esteem has many negative consequences. One is the tendency to create obstacles to your own performance. If you're concerned about an upcoming presentation, for example, you may neglect to prepare for it so that you can blame your poor performance on lack of preparation rather than lack of ability. Overemphasizing self-esteem can also lead you to deceive yourself. You ignore, or choose not to remember, your failures and shortcomings rather than using them as a motivation to improve. The study observes that you would be better off not playing games with yourself. Instead it recommends you accept yourself for who you are.

High self-esteem is not linked with success. Another study was unable to find any evidence that boosting self-esteem resulted in better job performance. The authors were unable to confirm other much-touted benefits of increased self-esteem, like having better relationships and making better impressions than those with low self-esteem.

Heidi Grant Halvorson, PhD, an author and the associate director for the Motivation Science Center at the Columbia University Business School, disputes the notion that high self-esteem predicts better performance or greater success. She debunks the teachings of over five thousand self-help books and challenges their premise that you can't possibly get ahead in life "unless you believe you are perfectly awesome."

Self-compassion may be more important than self-esteem. Halvorson believes self-compassion—not self-esteem—is the key to success. She defines self-compassion as "a willingness to look at your own mistakes and shortcomings with kindness and understanding—it's embracing the fact that to err is indeed human." Studies show that those who embrace self-compassion have higher levels of personal well-being, are more optimistic, and are less prone to anxiety and depression. Other studies demonstrate that those who are self-compassionate are more likely to achieve their goals than those who focus on boosting their self-esteem.

Why Many Self-Help Fixes Don't Work

Let's assume you're not aiming to become arrogant or delusional about how wonderful you are. You just want to achieve a healthy level of self-confidence and self-esteem. Will the quick and easy fixes offered in most self-help books, like positive mantras and visualization, actually work? Unfortunately, there is little evidence they will yield any meaningful benefits. Here's what studies show:

The causes of low self-esteem are largely out of our control. According to an exhaustive review of the research on self-esteem by Nicholas Emler at the London School of Economics, the single most important source of variation in self-esteem is genetic. Other important factors include upbringing: children of physically or emotionally abusive parents, or whose childhood was filled with family conflict and breakdown, are far more likely to suffer from low self-esteem. That doesn't mean it's impossible to raise your self-esteem. But it's unrealistic to think you can overcome such deep-rooted issues by repeating a few mantras.

Quick fixes can lower self-esteem. Studies have shown that the kind of quick-fix solutions proposed by many experts may actually make you feel worse. This makes perfect sense. You can't fool yourself. When I look into the mirror, I don't see Warren Buffett. If I repeat the mantra "I am as good as Warren Buffett," my brain is going to reject that statement as disconnected from reality. People with low self-esteem are unlikely to be persuaded by affirmations that so obviously depart from reality. Presumably, one of the manifestations of their low self-esteem is placing a low value on their own opinions.

Without some third-party affirmation, just repeating a mantra is unlikely to have a beneficial effect.

Visualizing your goal doesn't move you toward it. There is scant support for the premise that simply visualizing a goal makes it more likely you will achieve it. Unfortunately, this is the premise of many self-help programs. There is a critical difference between visualizing the results you want to achieve and visualizing the *actions* it will take to achieve those results. One study showed that students who visualized the tasks required to prepare for an exam did better than those who simply imagined the happiness they would feel upon receiving an A.

The Hot Coals Delusion

The self-help industry wants you to believe your lack of success is the consequence of not thinking positively. If you buy into this view, you are likely to blame yourself for events not within your control.

Nothing illustrates this issue better than a well-publicized debacle that occurred in July 2012. At an event sponsored by famous motivational speaker Anthony Robbins, called "Unleash the Power Within," twenty-one people were treated for burns caused when they were encouraged to walk barefoot over hot coals.

While the injury to their feet was painful, it paled in comparison to the damage to their pride and self-esteem. One participant was quoted as attributing his failure to the fact that he wasn't at his "peak state." This is the core of the problem. In order to be successful in sales (or in life), you need to focus on reality and stop blaming yourself for things over which you have little or no control.

Let's start with what can be learned about walking on hot coals. There is a considerable amount of research into the science of fire walking. It boils down to this: Wood that has burned down to coals is a poor conductor of heat. When a bed of burning coals is covered with an insulating layer of ash, you should be able to quickly scamper over it without suffering serious burns—regardless of your mindset.

A lot can go wrong, as is obvious from the Robbins event. The coals might not have reached the minimum required temperature of 1,000 degrees Fahrenheit. It is possible there was not a thin layer of ash over the coals, which would have provided the necessary insulation. There could have been excess water or bits of metal in the coals. Both increase thermal conductivity. The most obvious possibility is that the injured participants might have lingered too long instead of going as rapidly as possible over the coals.

Note that none of these problems relates to the state of mind of the participants. Yet those who got burned deemed themselves failures. They were blaming themselves for something that was not within their control. The problem was not their inability to "think positively." It was their misplaced reliance on positive thinking, which they naively believed could trump the laws of physics.

The Right Way to Think Positively

I am not suggesting you banish positive thoughts. I am proposing that those thoughts must be based in reality.

There is a meaningful distinction between positive *expectations* and positive *fantasies*. Positive expectations are based on applying past facts to future events. Suppose you are a salesperson with a track record of selling in a particular niche market. If your average sale is currently $10,000, and if, based on studying your market, you believe you can take steps to increase that average to $15,000 in a year or two, that's a positive expectation.

Positive fantasies are not based on a realistic assessment of the past. In addition, they exaggerate future possibilities. If you daydream about meeting a billionaire who spends a million dollars on your product or service, that's a positive fantasy.

There is considerable data supporting the view that having positive expectations can favorably impact your goals, while positive fantasies can negatively affect them. For example, one study asked graduating students to describe their beliefs about securing employment. Some questions focused on their expectations: "How probable do you think it is that you'll find an adequate position in your field?" Other questions measured how often the students had positive thoughts, images, or fantasies about graduating, getting a job, and transitioning into work life. Their answers were then compared to their actual experiences. It turned out that students with high expectations of success received more job offers and earned more money. Students who scored highly on experiencing positive fantasies had fewer job offers and earned less money.

This distinction is meaningful to salespeople. If you have a positive expectation based on past experience, you're more likely to achieve your goal. But a positive fantasy, like the dream of a million-dollar sale, may prevent you from engaging in the work necessary to achieve more realistic goals.

The Pragmatic Approach

I began this chapter by saying that successful salespeople are pragmatists. Now that you understand what doesn't work, the pragmatic approach is to focus on what does work. To increase your chances of success:

- Emphasize self-compassion rather than self-esteem.
- Base your goals on realistic expectations, not fantasies.
- Visualize actions, not results.
- Cultivate the traits and strategies explained in the rest of this book. They may not be as easy as the quick fixes, but they're based on solid evidence.

WHAT'S THE POINT?

Quick fixes are distractions from the hard work it takes to succeed.

CHAPTER 2

Honesty

If you are honest, people may cheat you. Be honest anyway.
—Mother Teresa

There's no shortage of anecdotal data about the negative impressions the general public has of salespeople. One survey of 2,705 corporate buyers across six countries yielded depressing feedback. Over 47 percent of US-based buyers said they would not be proud to be called a salesperson. One UK buyer noted that after dealing with a salesperson he felt "conned" and "cheated." Only 53 percent of those responding rated their experience with salespeople as good. Some of the more colorful observations were that salespeople were "cut-throat," "irritating," "like sharks," "lower than pond scum," "leeches," and "leg-humping dogs" who "will promise their first-born to get the sale."

To be successful in sales, you need to be aware of this negative mindset. Fortunately, it should not be difficult to change it by adopting some basic values. Let's start with honesty.

Honesty Is Admired

Venture capitalists who responded to one survey indicated that honesty was the most important personal trait for an entrepreneur. Other surveys concluded that honesty is the most admired trait for business leaders.

In the excellent book, *The Leadership Challenge*, the authors set forth a basic principle, which you should frame and put on your desk: "If you don't believe in the messenger, you won't believe the message."

Honesty has collateral benefits unrelated to meeting your sales quota. You will experience closer, more meaningful relationships with loved ones, friends, and colleagues. You will attract higher quality, more trustworthy people in your life. Your physical and mental health will improve. You will be less stressed. Others will trust you more.

Women Have the "Honesty Edge"

Women have an innate advantage in the honesty department. In one survey, male and female financial services professionals were asked whether they would engage in insider trading (the purchase or sale of a security while in possession of nonpublic information) if they stood to make $10 million and had no chance of getting caught. Among those expressing a willingness to engage in this illegal conduct (which would clearly harm investors on the other side of the trade) were 19 percent of men but only 10 percent of women.

A more comprehensive study was conducted by Roger Steare, who is a visiting professor of organizational ethics and corporate philosopher in residence at the Cass Business School in London. Steare constructed a "moral DNA test" that was taken by over sixty thousand participants from two hundred countries. The purpose of the test was to gauge the level of morality of the participants, measuring traits like honesty and competency.

The test indicated that women are more moral than men. They were more likely than men to base their decisions on how they impacted others. Women over age thirty were found to be the most honest.

According to Steare, "What this shows is that when it comes to work, men have to grow up, put their ego to one side and show some humility and compassion—qualities they all too often have in their personal lives but put to one side when they walk into the office."

How do you want your customer to perceive you? As someone who acts solely in your own self-interest? Or as someone who is genuinely concerned about the customer's best interest?

Gender-Based Perceptions of Honesty

Your gender and speech patterns can significantly affect the perception others have of your honesty. A study by Marilyn Boltz, a professor of psychology at Haverford College, and her colleagues at the University of Maryland and Yale University, found that women are generally perceived to lie less than men and to tell different kinds of lies. Participants in the study listened to a taped conversation between a dating couple and were asked whether the responses were true or lies. Here's one of the conversations:

Jim: Were you happy with the steak?

Claire: Yeah, it was really good. Was it your own recipe for the marinade?

Jim: Yeah, it was. It's one I've been trying to perfect over the years.

The most interesting finding in the study was the expectation of the type of lies told by men and women. The expectation was that men would tell lies likely to benefit themselves, while women would lie to benefit others. Jim's claim that he had been working on the recipe "for years" was thought by most of the participants to be untruthful. Claire's statement that the steak was "really good" was also considered likely to be a lie. Jim's "lie" was self-aggrandizing. Claire's was intended to protect his male ego. The issue here is not whether Jim or Claire actually lied. It's far more consequential: If you are a man involved in sales, you should be aware of an additional burden you may confront when dealing with a potential customer. Your gender alone may predispose your customer to believe you are not being honest, even if that perception is inaccurate. In order to overcome this perception, you need to be scrupulously careful not to overstate or misrepresent anything about your product or service.

To succeed in sales, you must not only be honest, you must be perceived as being honest.

Improve Your Credibility

Now that you understand the importance of both honesty and the perception of honesty, here's a simple exercise you can do. You will need to work with a partner and use an audio or video recorder. With the recorder running, have your partner ask you a series of questions about your service or product. Answer them honestly. When you play back the recording, listen carefully to your responses. Do they seem slow and labored? Is the pitch of your voice higher than when you engage in normal conversation? You should be aware that these tendencies might cause your prospects to believe you are not being truthful—even though this is not the case. If your natural speech pattern is to respond slowly or to raise the pitch of your voice, you may need to retrain yourself. Certain nonverbal signals have also been shown to be perceived as indicating lack of candor. These include blinking, hand shrugs, pupil dilation, and self-touching.

Put the Customer First

By keeping your focus on doing the right thing for your prospect, not only will you be acting honestly, but you can also be assured you will be perceived as honest. Here's an example.

What if you went into your local Ford dealer looking for a truck for a very specific need, like hauling a certain kind of cargo. Instead of showing you the Ford truck closest to your requirements, the salesperson tells you, "We don't have anything suitable for that specific purpose. I know Chevrolet has a truck that will do exactly what you want. Have you checked it out?"

This scenario takes a vivid imagination. I suspect it is a rare occurrence. What if that was your experience? How would you perceive the Ford salesperson? Do you think you would tell that story to your friends? Would you be inclined to give that person your business in the future? The Ford salesperson might lose one sale in the short term, but would reap the rewards of that honesty for years to come.

This example might remind you of the iconic scene from *Miracle on 34th Street*. Macy's Santa Claus refused to follow the directions of his boss to steer customers to Macy's products. Instead, he sent one customer to another store for a fire engine Macy's didn't carry. Then he committed an unthinkable act of disloyalty. He told the mother of a child that Macy's rival, Gimbels, had superior skates and suggested she go there and buy them for her daughter. This simple act of candor had consequences no one could have imagined. Macy's received so much positive publicity that Gimbels instituted a similar referral policy. All because of one selfless act. The story is fictional, but the moral is compelling.

I am familiar with the practices of many brokers and advisors in the securities industry. It's unfortunate that so many of them act in a way that suits their own economic interest and is harmful to the financial goals of their clients. It's not a coincidence that some of the major players went bankrupt or were reorganized after the 2008 financial crisis.

Putting the customer first is not just an abstract ethical principle. It's good business. Adopting this core value will help you become a successful salesperson. You will also sleep well at night.

WHAT'S THE POINT?

Both the reality and the perception of being totally honest are critical to your success in sales.

CHAPTER 3

Sincerity

Sincerity makes the very least person to be of more value than
the most talented hypocrite.
—Charles Spurgeon

I don't agree with French diplomat and novelist Jean Giraudoux. He supposedly said, "The secret of success is sincerity. Once you can fake that you've got it made." My views are more in line with an insightful report prepared by the Arthur W. Page Society. It found that "authenticity will be the coin of the realm for successful corporations and for those who lead them." Authenticity, or sincerity, will also be the "coin of the realm" for salespeople who want to achieve their goals.

I distinguish sincerity from honesty. Honesty is about how you represent the product or service. Telling someone the used car you are trying to sell has never been in an accident would be honest, assuming that was true. Sincerity is about how you represent yourself—being genuinely yourself, without pretending to be something or someone you're not. If you are selling life insurance, telling the client you really care about her and her family and want to do the right thing for them could be either sincere or insincere. If it's true, it is sincere. If your focus is really on maximizing your sales commission, it's insincere.

For many years, I was a trial lawyer in New York City. This is not a profession for the faint of heart. Lawyers will do and say almost anything to persuade juries and judges of the righteousness of their clients' cases. I often observed out-of-state lawyers who tried to "fit in" by becoming instant New Yorkers, praising the Yankees and Mets and referring to their New York roots. It rarely worked. Their pandering (and lack of sincerity) was obvious. They looked foolish and lost credibility.

The Danger of Being Perceived as Insincere

To be successful in sales, you need to be sincere and also to be perceived as being sincere. One study found that clients who perceived their real estate agents as being sincere (by evaluating body language, sincere smiles, voice tone and facial expressions) were more likely to feel satisfied with the service provided by those agents.

Another study found that apologies given by those involved in romantic relationships that were perceived as more sincere made the recipient of the apology feel more satisfied and less angry.

Don't underestimate the positive impact of being perceived as sincere.

Embrace Who You Are

The benefits of embracing who you are and not trying to be someone else are illustrated by this true story of a trial held in a small town in South Dakota. The plaintiff was seeking damages for a traumatic brain injury suffered in a trucking accident. The defendant was represented by hometown lawyers. The plaintiff brought in "big city" lawyers from Chicago. The defendant's lawyers made much of this fact by deriding the presence of "fancy, high-powered" attorneys.

The plaintiff's lawyers could have responded by trying to downplay or avoid mentioning their "big city" status. Instead, they embraced it. They explained to the jury that they would ask them to place the same value on this injury as a jury in Chicago would award and that it should make no difference where the injury was suffered or where the lawyers were from. The jury returned one of the largest verdicts ever awarded in South Dakota. In post-trial interviews, some of the jurors said that bringing lawyers in from a big city gave the case more importance in their minds.

Speak from Your Heart

Sincerity is something a good salesperson needs in abundance. It should never be faked. It's a quality we all have. We just need to use it and to be perceived as having it.

After Apple co-founder Steve Jobs died, there was much attention focused on a commencement address he gave at Stanford University on June 12, 2005. At the time, he had been diagnosed with pancreatic cancer. His talk showed a kinder, more compassionate side

Jobs spoke about his life in intensely personal terms. He discussed the impact of his humiliating, public firing from Apple. His most powerful observations were the lessons he learned about living life to the fullest as he was confronting his own mortality. There was no doubt he was speaking from the heart.

Sincerity is something a good salesperson needs in abundance. It should never be faked. It's a quality we all have. We just need to use it and to be perceived as having it.

WHAT'S THE POINT?

Embrace who you are and speak from your heart.

CHAPTER 4

Grit

Whether it's the pioneer in the Conestoga wagon or someone
coming here in the 1920s from southern Italy, there was this
idea in America that if you worked hard and you showed real
grit, that you could be successful.
—Dominic Randolph

The good news is that great salespeople are not born
that way. The bad news is that becoming successful in
sales takes a tremendous amount of motivation, hard work,
and perseverance.

What Is Grit?

Just because two people have the same intelligence, it's
unlikely they both will achieve the same level of success.

One study attempted to isolate the ingredient that causes outstanding success that cannot be accounted for by intelligence. The study looked at many traits, including creativity, emotional intelligence, charisma, self-confidence, emotional stability, and attractiveness. The one quality that stood out, across all fields (including sales), was "grit." The authors of the study found that across different disciplines, grit was as important a factor in accomplishing goals as talent.

What is "grit"? It's defined in the study simply as "perseverance and passion for long-term goals." But real grit entails working toward a goal even in the face of adversity. I like to think of it as perseverance on steroids.

The Critical Role of Grit

An extensive study on the relationship of grit to success found that those with high grit scores appeared to have greater ability to reach long-term goals, like pursuing higher education. They were also less likely to be frequent career changers.

Students who scored higher on the grit scale had higher grade point averages than less "gritty" students. Here's an important finding: significantly higher grit was associated with *lower* SAT scores. The authors theorize that individuals who are not as intelligent as their peers compensate by working harder and showing more determination.

Higher grit scores predicted advancement to higher rounds in spelling bee competition. Those with high grit scores outperformed their competitors in the final rounds. Higher grit scores also predicted who would get to the final round when age was held as a constant. The authors concluded that students with a lot of grit simply put in more hours. Hard work was rewarded with better performance.

While there is no positive relationship between grit and intelligence, those with higher grit were more likely to achieve success in their chosen careers.

There is considerable evidence that follow-through is the essence of grit. One study of college students demonstrated that follow-through is a better predictor of achieving a leadership position in college than all other variables, including SAT scores. Here's the overall conclusion of the authors of this study: "Given that college grades are only modestly correlated with adult success . . . we wonder whether follow-through or, as we prefer to call it, grit, may in fact matter more than IQ to eventual success in life."

This study has serious ramifications. It debunks the myth that we are born with the "success gene." It's not genetics that accounts for success, but rather what we do with what we are given.

Outliers and Grit

There is ample additional support for the importance of grit. In his seminal book *Outliers: The Story of Success*, Malcolm Gladwell focuses on this issue: What are the traits of highly successful people? He concludes there are some factors over which we have no control, like background, opportunities, mentoring, and timing. But his key finding is that elite performers (he calls them "outliers") share one trait: they have put in ten thousand hours of hard work. Gladwell quotes this finding by neurologist Daniel Levitin: "The emerging picture from such studies is that ten thousand hours of practice is required to achieve the level of mastery associated with being a world-class expert—in anything."

Let's put ten thousand hours of hard work in perspective. According to Gladwell, "To become a chess grandmaster also seems to take about ten years. (Only the legendary Bobby Fisher got to that elite level in less than that amount of time: it took him nine years.) And what's ten years? Well, it's roughly how long it takes to put in ten thousand hours of hard practice. Ten thousand hours is the magic number of greatness."

Keep in mind that Gladwell is talking about what it takes to be an "outlier," someone who is truly exceptional. Most of us will never reach that level and don't need to. It won't take us ten thousand hours of deliberate practice to be successful in our chosen occupation.

K. Anders Ericsson, a professor of psychology at Florida State University, reinforces Gladwell's view of the importance of hard work in achieving success. Ericsson notes that the performance difference between professional musicians and serious amateur musicians can be explained by the amount of time spent practicing. The best experts put in ten thousand hours by age twenty, compared to only two thousand hours for the amateurs. These findings relate directly to the conclusions about the prominence of grit. The key predictive factor is the amount of "deliberate practice," which is defined as focusing relentlessly on your weaknesses and finding ways to improve them. Simply spending a set number of hours putting in time is not enough.

We Control Our Destiny

The idea that we (and not our DNA) have control over our destinies is critical. It finds further support in studies of geniuses, like Mozart. David Brooks, op-ed columnist for the *New York Times*, summarized this research. He concluded that genius is not "a divine spark." Instead, it is a function of the ability to focus on a goal consistently, over a long period of time, and to rigorously concentrate on practicing one's craft and improving one's skills.

Here are some suggestions for developing grit and making it a focal point of your efforts to improve your sales:

Don't get discouraged. True grit means having an indomitable spirit. Being rejected is part of the life of everyone involved in sales. In order to succeed, you need to keep going when others would throw in the towel.

Persevere. . . to a point. Especially in high-level sales, getting a positive response can take months or even years of effort. One survey of sales executives found that over 80 percent of sales did not close until the fifth call.

However, knowing when to give up on a sale is also important. Your time has a value. If you continue to focus on customers who are unlikely to buy what you're selling, you are not going to have the time necessary to find those who will. Blindly accepting the mantra to "never give up" can impede your sales success, if taken to an extreme.

Work harder. For many years I have tried cases with the assistance of a small law firm located in a city in western Massachusetts. I interviewed a number of firms who wanted to associate with me. All of them worked in nicer offices, had better legal backgrounds, and could deploy far more support services than the firm I chose. I selected this firm because the lawyer told me the following when I met him: "I may not be as smart as the other lawyers you are interviewing, and we are not located in a big city. But I can tell you this: you won't find anyone who will outwork us or be more committed to winning your cases." I never regretted basing my decision on his commitment to work harder than everyone else.

Refine your skills. Attend sales conferences and continuing education seminars. Some fields, like legal, medical, insurance, and investment advisory services, offer limitless possibilities to expand your knowledge and even achieve advanced designations or degrees. If you want to have grit, you need to push yourself to the limit by pursuing courses that make you better qualified to sell your product or service than your competitors.

Associate with other successful salespeople. Look for a mentor and offer to mentor others. Never stop learning about effective sales strategies.

A Story of True Grit

Here's a real story of true grit. I changed the names and some details to protect the privacy of those involved.

Norma had a very inauspicious beginning to her life. She was born in Korea. Her biological father was stationed there as a US soldier, and her mother was a native Korean. Norma was left on the doorstep of a Catholic orphanage.

Shortly after she arrived there, a young American couple came to the orphanage. They had been approved for the adoption of a baby girl named Mary. The adoptive father was enlisted in the Army and stationed in Korea, and he and his wife were about to return to the States. They had no children and were moved by the number of unwanted children in Korean orphanages. The children least likely to be adopted by Koreans were of mixed race, a characteristic that was highly stigmatized.

As the new parents were leaving the orphanage with Mary, a nun approached them. She was holding Norma, who was obviously malnourished. The nun told them the orphanage did not have the resources to look after Norma. She begged them to adopt her as well. Although they had little money or prospects, the parents left the orphanage with not one, but two adopted babies.

Norma was raised in a loving home in central Oklahoma. Her new parents never had much money, but instilled in her basic values of hard work, kindness, and spirituality. She showed promise in school, but had a rebellious streak that made raising her a challenge.

When Norma graduated from high school, her parents couldn't afford to send her to a four-year college. She went to a small community college instead. After completing her studies there, she took out student loans and transferred to a university. When she was nineteen and still a student, she married an engineering student she met at school.

After college, Norma took a job as a chemist with a drug company and supported her husband while he completed his engineering degree. She found her job boring and unfulfilling. She had always wanted to be a doctor. Her husband was less than enthused about this potential change in her career. Norma applied to several medical schools but was rejected by all of them. She didn't give up.

The following year, when she was in her late twenties, Norma was finally accepted at a medical school that was part of the military. She was required to enlist in the military and commit to paying for her medical school education with service in the armed forces. She moved from Oklahoma to the District of Columbia alone. She had to borrow from friends to make the move and pay her initial expenses. She and her husband divorced during her first year of medical school. She persevered, and four years later she was awarded her medical degree.

Norma did an internship and was then deployed to remote foreign bases, where she was a medical officer to soldiers. Each deployment was a new experience, requiring her to adjust to her circumstances. She was accepted as a resident in an orthopedic surgery program. After five more arduous years, she completed her residency, passed her boards, and married another military doctor. Along the way, she learned how to shoot a gun and dig latrines as part of her overall training. No one cut her any slack.

Today she is a high-ranking officer in the military reserves. Here's the best part of the story: she and her husband adopted two children from China.

Norma has true grit. So do her remarkable adoptive parents.

The harsh reality is that there are no shortcuts. Hard work, perseverance or grit, staying the course, meeting challenges, overcoming adversity, learning from your mistakes, and following through are not easy traits to cultivate. But they will put you on a path to the road of success that is honest, straightforward, and built on a strong foundation.

WHAT'S THE POINT?

There is no substitute for hard work, determination, and perseverance.

CHAPTER 5

Empathy

I find that if you use empathy, and from that place, ask great
questions, you can really find out what is most important for your
prospective clients or current clients.
—Jeffrey J. Ulmer

Empathy is the ability to feel and understand another
person's situation and communicate that feeling. We
can be empathetic only when we let go of our thoughts and
agendas and focus intently on others. Most people don't
want us to fix their problems. They just want to know we
have genuinely listened to them and really heard what they
are saying.

Therapists agree that empathy is critical to a successful
relationship. One therapist described the following steps to

good empathetic communication. As you review them, keep in mind how applicable they are to establishing an emotional connection in your sales efforts.

- Listen without interrupting.
- Think about the feelings of the other person.
- Mirror back those feelings to be sure you understand them.
- Demonstrate an understanding of those feelings.
- Offer to try to work out the problem together.

An Example of Empathy

Here's a compelling example demonstrating the power of showing empathy. For many years when I was practicing law, I worked with a lawyer from a small town on the East Coast. I enjoyed working with him, and not just because of his superior intellect and integrity. He had a wonderfully understated personality, which was very effective in and out of the courtroom. He was unfailingly polite to everyone, including his adversaries.

One evening he told me he was being considered for a coveted (and very competitive) position as a judge. A number of lawyers desperately wanted this job. My friend was ultimately appointed by the governor, subject to confirmation by the state legislature. He told me the confirmation was by no means assured. To buttress the possibility of an affirmative vote, appointees often ask pillars of the community to testify to their stellar legal and personal virtues. There is no shortage of people (especially lawyers) eager to testify and curry favor with a potential new judge.

Several months later, I learned that my friend had been confirmed. I called to congratulate him and asked who appeared to testify on his behalf. He told me he had asked only one person to appear. I was curious. Was it the president of the local bar association? Another judge who thought highly of him? Maybe a former legislator, known to members of the judicial committee? It turned out to be none of the above.

The person he chose was one of the security guards who was assigned to the courtroom where he tried most of his cases. The guard nervously told the committee he was just a blue-collar worker and had never spoken in a public forum before, much less testified before a congressional committee. He said the appointee was respected and liked by all of the personnel who worked in the courthouse. He was always respectful to them and asked about their well-being and their families. The guard concluded by saying that while he wasn't competent to evaluate the appointee's legal skills, "juries really like him."

The chair of the congressional committee set the tone for the balance of the hearings. He told the guard that his father was also a blue-collar worker and that he had nothing but respect for the fact that the guard overcame his fears and testified so honestly. He then said that nothing was more important to the judicial selection process than the way judges treat members of the public, regardless of their social status.

My friend was appointed by a unanimous vote. He is a credit to the judiciary. He closed the "sale." He was able to empathize with the feelings of the congressional committee.

The Role of Empathy in Sales

Studies have shown that empathy is a significant personality trait that is desirable in salespeople. It is a critical component of interaction between a buyer and a seller.

Empathetic listeners are sensitive to what is spoken and implied. They hear the points the other person is making and acknowledge them. They are open to other points of view. Empathetic listeners ask questions to be sure their understanding is accurate. Both verbally and nonverbally, they indicate their interest in the feelings being expressed.

The late Stephen Covey, author of *The 7 Habits of Highly Effective People*, considered one of the most important habits to be empathy. He referred to it as the habit to "seek first to understand." When you listen to others empathically, your sole goal is to "see the world the way they see the world, you understand their paradigm, you understand how they feel. . . . You listen with your ears, but you also, and more importantly, listen with your eyes and with your heart. You listen for feeling, for meaning. You listen for behavior. You use your right brain as well as your left. You sense, you intuit, you feel."

Empathy and Charisma

When you adopt these habits, you become "remarkably charismatic." That's the conclusion of Jeff Haden, a prolific author of business and investing books. Charismatic people are those who are able to develop meaningful relationships with others, in both their business and personal lives. Other people are attracted to them because those around them feel important and valued. According to Liz Wendling, an author and sales coach, top salespeople have sales charisma. She describes them as "inspirational, passionate, self-confident, insightful, ambitious, visionary and dynamic." These traits attract prospects.

Here are some of the traits of charismatic people:

- They listen very closely instead of dominating the conversation.

- They focus intently on the person speaking, without any distractions.

- They have humility and a self-deprecating sense of humor.

- They make others feel good about themselves by talking up to them.

Empathy Tips

There is bad and good news for developing more empathy. The bad news: there is support for the view that our ability to empathize with others may be part of our DNA. One study showed that those with certain genetic variants of the receptor for a brain chemical known as oxytocin may have a predisposition to be empathetic.

The good news is that everyone can develop an ability to be more empathetic. Here are some tips:

Listen. You can't demonstrate empathy unless you understand the emotions of your prospective customer. These feelings can be expressed in words or in nonverbal gestures. Be sensitive to all cues.

Feel. Recently, my wife cut herself while opening a can. The gash was pretty deep and bled profusely. I helped her stop the bleeding, cleaned up the cut, and bandaged the wound. I could intensely feel her pain. Sometimes we pay lip service to understanding the feelings of others ("I can feel your pain"), but we don't really mean it. We remain consumed with our own agenda. If you want to be empathetic, try to *really* experience the feelings of your customers, just as if they were your own.

Don't argue. Rejection is the daily grist of most salespeople. Our normal tendency is to try to change the minds of those who disagree with us. Resist this temptation. It is entirely possible that their views are correct. Maybe your product or service is not suitable for your prospective customer. Maybe better options are available from your competitors. In my experience, when others have strongly held views, I am rarely successful in changing their minds, even when their views are demonstrably wrong. Many salespeople assume that a customer who doesn't want to buy from them must be mistaken. At the very least, you need to fully understand the customer's point of view before engaging in any further discussion.

WHAT'S THE POINT?

When you focus on becoming more empathetic,
your sales will increase.

CHAPTER 6

Self-Awareness

We don't know where our first impressions come
from or precisely what they mean, so we don't always
appreciate their fragility.
—Malcolm Gladwell

Successful salespeople are keenly self-aware. While the Internet has dramatically increased interactions via computer, many sales transactions still involve face-to-face meetings. Successful salespeople need to be aware of the first impression they make. Otherwise they may risk losing the sale before they have the opportunity to discuss the merits of their products or services.

We Make Judgments in Nanoseconds

How long do you think it takes others to form an impression of you? How about a tenth of a second? That's the conclusion of a study by Janine Willis and Alexander Todorov, published in *Psychological Science*. Undergraduate students from Princeton University were shown pictures of male and female actors and were asked to give an opinion about various traits of the person in each picture. The researchers found that exposure time as small as one-tenth of a second was enough for the participants to form an opinion about important traits. This might not seem startling if the only trait being evaluated was attractiveness. It wasn't. The participants also formed views about trustworthiness, likeability, and competence.

I experienced this phenomenon firsthand when I gave a lecture to trial lawyers in New York City. Approximately two hundred lawyers were in attendance. As you might expect, they were an intelligent—if somewhat jaded—and very savvy audience. Naturally, they were concerned about the impression they made on juries.

After I introduced myself, I said, "Before I start, I want to ask you some questions about myself." I called for a show of hands: Do I vacation at an expensive resort in the

South of France, or do I prefer more basic accommodations like Club Med? Do I prefer wine or beer? Am I affectionate with my children or distant and aloof? Almost everyone in the audience had an opinion. The majority of the attendees thought I preferred the expensive resort and wine and that I was distant and aloof with my children. They were wrong, but that's beside the point. Just by looking at me on the podium and hearing me introduce myself, they had formed definite impressions. We all do this all the time.

Factors Affecting First Impressions

Studies have shown the effects that short and long hairstyles can have on someone's first impression of a woman. A woman's short hair may make her appear confident and outgoing. Longer tresses are perceived as sexy and affluent.

The same study showed the impact of men's hairstyles. Men with short, front-flip hair (like Matt LeBlanc) are perceived as confident and sexy. Men with medium-length, side-parted hair are perceived as intelligent and affluent.

A 2012 survey showed that two in five Americans would not go on a second date with someone who has crooked teeth. Attractive teeth were also associated with making a positive first impression, being successful, having a good personality, and being trustworthy.

One study looked at the effect of clothing on first impressions. Women wearing skirt suits were perceived to be more confident than women wearing trouser suits. Men were rated more positively on traits relating to confidence, success, trustworthiness, and flexibility if they wore custom suits rather than off-the-rack. The authors of the study concluded that "people are judged on their overall head-to-toe appearance, and the fundamental role that dress style plays in creating a positive first impression cannot be underestimated."

Another study looked at the impact of an applicant's attire during a job interview. Participants were asked to read a description of a fictitious job applicant, including qualifications and clothing. The attire of the "applicant" was described as either business casual; standard, off-the-rack suit; or custom suit. It showed that casual attire caused participants to rate the applicant as being less competent. Applicants dressed in more formal attire were more likely to be offered an upper-level management position.

I recently had an experience that validated this conclusion. I appeared on a television program and decided to dress casually. Instead of a suit and tie, I wore a blazer with a turtleneck shirt. The other guest was a woman who was dressed very formally. She disagreed with my investment advice, but I was confident the research supported my views and undermined hers. After the segment aired, I asked a friend, who is a well-known director of television commercials, to evaluate my presentation. He told me he found the other guest more credible. He couldn't restate our various positions, but he said he was influenced by the difference in our attire. She seemed "more professional." I never made that mistake again.

The way you shake hands can have a significant effect on the first impression you make. In one study, four trained "coders" (two men and two women) shook hands with 112 participants. After each shake, the coders rated the physical characteristics of the handshake and their impression of the participant's personality. The authors of the study found that a firm handshake conveyed traits of extraversion and emotional expressiveness. Those with firm handshakes were also deemed unlikely to be shy or neurotic.

The Beauty Premium

If you are fortunate enough to be viewed as attractive, you

definitely have an edge. According to an article in the *New York Times*, attractive people earn more, marry higher-earning spouses, and even get better mortgage terms!

Being attractive may give women a special edge. According to Dr. Catherine Hakim, a British sociologist, women who have the "beauty premium" earn significantly more than those without it.

A comprehensive study looked at whether salespeople making presentations to physicians were more successful if they were attractive. The authors found that perceived physical attractiveness had a meaningful, positive impact on sales. The effect became smaller over longer-term relationships. The study also found that attractive people were perceived to be better communicators, more likeable, greater in expertise, and more trustworthy than their less attractive colleagues.

An essential component of sales success is recognizing that your appearance and the first impression you make can be important factors in your ability to close sales.

WHAT'S THE POINT?

Be aware of the first impression others have of you.
You may not get a second chance.

Part Two

Strategies of Successful Salespeople

CHAPTER 7

Understand the Power of Emotional Connections

The fact is that great musical pieces take and hold the stage because they provide great emotional experiences.
—Sarah Caldwell

When you meet a prospect for the first time, your goal is clear: you want to make a sale. Ironically, rigidly adhering to that goal is likely to have the opposite effect: you are *less* likely to make the sale. Here's a new goal: *you want to make an emotional connection.* If you do, your chances of making a sale increase exponentially.

Compelling research indicates that over 50 percent of a buying decision is based on emotions. Businesses that optimize emotional connections significantly outperform those that don't, in both gross margin and revenues. The evidence is overwhelming that emotionally engaging your customers yields significant returns. According to the Gallup Organization, "If you don't make an emotional connection with customers, then satisfaction is worthless."

Many salespeople are not aware of the power of making an emotional connection. For them, a sales conversation is a "data dump." It involves extolling the virtues of whatever they are selling. This is a fundamental mistake. You will appreciate this better when you understand what our brains do when presented with information.

How the Brain Processes Information

What determines whether a potential customer will remember the information you present? Brain capacity is not the issue. Our brains have the capacity to store an enormous amount of information. By one estimate, your brain has enough storage capacity to hold three million hours of TV shows.

The capacity to store information is one thing. Actually storing it is quite another. In his book *How the Brain Learns*, Dr. David Sousa, a consultant in educational neuroscience, explains that everything you experience through your senses is processed through the sensory register of the brain. The information is then routed to a temporary holding area in short-term memory. If your brain perceives the information as meaningful, it will be permanently stored in long-term memory. Otherwise, it gets dumped.

How long we retain information in short-term memory varies with the type of information being processed. Sousa gives the example of hearing a siren while sitting in a classroom. Your brain processes this information and recognizes it as a source of possible danger. However, as the sound becomes faint, you will refocus your attention on the lecture. After a relatively short period of time, you may not even remember hearing the siren.

The Limitations of Short-Term Memory

Ask a friend to help you with this experiment. He or she is going to give you strings of random numbers from zero through nine. You will try to repeat them back in sequence. For example, your friend could start with two digits: "Seven, four." You would repeat back "Seven, four." Then your friend might say "Six, zero, three." You would repeat those numbers back. Each time, increase the number of digits by one. The object is to see how long a series of numbers you can remember.

You may be surprised by the results. The average person's short-term memory has the ability to retain only seven numbers. The same is true with letters.

I tried this experiment with three of the smartest people I know. Their jobs involve analyzing vast amounts of data. They are all under thirty years old. They have degrees in finance or statistics. Their number-crunching abilities are extraordinary. Two of them were able to repeat back ten digits. The other one got nine right before faltering.

Think about this for a moment. These are people whose lives revolve around making sense of complex information. Yet the best of them could only retain ten digits in the correct order. A computer can instantly retrieve all stored information. Your brain is different.

When our short-term memory gets overloaded, it tends to retain information it can associate with data already held in long-term memory. For many of us, September 11, 2001, when the World Trade Center and the Pentagon were struck by terrorists, is a date we will never forget. It is permanently stored in long-term memory. If another meaningful event occurred on that date—say, the birth of a friend's baby—we would find it quite easy to remember what day it happened. But if the birth occurred on some other day that otherwise held no special significance, we probably would not be able to recall the date as easily.

Emotions Trump Facts

Think of the brain as a giant funnel. Every minute of your waking day, you are confronted with all kinds of information. You hear sounds, smell odors (positive and negative), touch things, see things, talk with other people, and make thousands of judgments. The aggregate amount of data your brain is coping with could be as much as ten trillion bits per second! Your brain needs to prioritize, or it will become overwhelmed.

How does the brain prioritize information? By giving it a well-defined pecking order. Certain types of information get more of your brain's attention. That's where the emotions come in.

At the top of the pecking order is information that signals possible danger. Picture yourself walking down a deserted street late at night. You are thinking about an important presentation and how to position your points to make the greatest impact. Suddenly you hear footsteps behind you. Your brain senses danger. It dumps all the other data it was processing and focuses on survival. This response is lightning fast.

The brain's second highest priority is processing other types of emotional data. That includes any information you respond to with anger, joy, sadness, fear, or other strong feelings.

Factual data is at the bottom of the brain's pecking order. The brain responds far more slowly when it is required to integrate facts, compare them with past experiences, and interpret them in a rational manner.

Your brain not only processes emotional and factual data differently, it stores them differently. Emotional and factual memories are stored in separate parts of the brain. The factual memory area holds information that you don't feel strongly about, such as what you had for dinner last night. Events that triggered an emotional reaction, such as a marriage proposal or a breakup, are stored in your emotional memory.

The brain "likes" emotional information, both positive and negative. That's why emotional memories are so vivid. The victim of a traumatic attack can relive all of the horrific details by revisiting the scene of the crime, even many years later. The same level of recall occurs with positive emotional events.

Emotional Memories Are Long-Lasting

About fifteen years ago, my wife and I took my mom, who was then in her eighties, on a cruise to Alaska. I am not very adventurous, but my wife is an avid hiker and nature lover. She lobbied hard for the three of us to take a guided river rafting tour. I resisted because of my own fears and concern for my mother, who was very apprehensive at the prospect. We all talked it over and decided to take the risk. We were outfitted in rain ponchos and safety vests. We all looked ridiculous. As we attempted to board the wobbly craft, my mom said, "I'm sure I am the only eighty-three-year-old dumb enough to do this."

I can remember every moment of that trip as if it were yesterday. It was beyond exhilarating. The scenery was spectacular. I recall passing a breathtaking waterfall. The sheer adventure of running the rapids in an unstable vessel was unlike anything I—and certainly my mom—had ever experienced. Always alert to the possibility of making a profit, the ship stationed photographers at various points along the banks of the river. They took stunning pictures. We bought every one.

Even after all these years, whenever I feel a little depressed, I take out those pictures and let the memories of that experience come flooding back to me. My mom never looked so happy. Shortly before she died, I asked her to tell me some of the most memorable experiences of her life. The rafting adventure was near the top of the list. I can't recall the date we took that trip, or even the year, but I remember the experience like it was yesterday.

I am sure you can relate my story to many experiences in your own life, both positive (birth of a child, special trip, first job interview, graduation) and negative (death of a loved one, terrible accident, or other traumatic event). These experiences leave an indelible impression. Your brain stores—and instantly recalls—powerful emotional experiences. That's why you can forget where you put your glasses ten minutes ago but vividly recall your high school prom.

One researcher described the high memory retention of emotional events as akin to having them "photographically etched in the brain." Even more surprising, this recall ability, unlike other brain functions, does not appear to decline with age. It appears to be timeless. The ability to retain emotional connections can even survive other impairments to the brain. A study in Japan found that participants with Alzheimer's disease were still able to recall information that made an emotional connection.

Conveying Information the Brain Will Retain

If you convey information that the brain delegates to the lowest rung of the processing ladder, don't expect your listener to understand—or even have any interest in—what you are saying. You need the emotional connection to make an impression.

Here's an example. We are all concerned about our national debt. However, few of us can appreciate the enormity of debt expressed in trillions of dollars. A national debt clock near Times Square makes this abstract number personal. It computes the portion of the debt attributable to every family in the United States. By translating the debt into your family's "share," the clock turns factual data into emotional data.

In sales, the challenge is to provide information that will get the brain's attention and be selected for storage in long-term memory. The only way to do that is by making an emotional connection. This is where most salespeople fail.

Many years ago, I spoke at a conference of insurance salespeople held in Las Vegas. At a dinner of agents and potential clients, one of the agents dominated the conversation with an extensive recitation of the merits of his insurance offerings. His knowledge of facts and figures was encyclopedic. He rattled off a wealth of historical data that fully supported his point of view.

I met with him after the dinner and asked him if this was his normal approach to sales. He was very offended by my use of the word "sales." He explained that he was not in "sales." He was an "educator." His job was to "educate" potential clients by giving them the information they need to make a decision. He then stated dismissively that what they did with the information he provided was entirely up to them. If they weren't smart enough to appreciate the value he provided, they were free to go elsewhere. "Some customers," he said, "just don't get it."

I asked the prospects who attended the dinner how they reacted to the presentation. The prevailing response was that they tuned the agent out shortly after he started reciting data. Information that fails to elicit passion or an emotional reaction in the listener is likely to fall on deaf ears. It probably won't be retained in short-term memory, much less be given a coveted spot in long-term memory.

What if the agent had begun by asking, "What role do you think insurance could play in relieving your anxiety?" I suspect most people have the same concern: they are worried they will die or become disabled and leave their family in dire straits. That fear is stored as vividly as the memory of a traumatic event. If you are an insurance agent, address those fears and you will make a powerful emotional connection. You will also be in a much better position to suggest a product that addresses the prospect's concerns—and make a sale.

Now you know why emotional connection is so important. The next few chapters will show you how to make the connection.

WHAT'S THE POINT?

Understanding how the brain processes information will help you craft a message that will resonate with prospective customers.

CHAPTER 8

Connect with Your Customers

The future belongs to those who make emotional connections with their customers.
—Diane Berenbaum

A s indicated in Chapter 7, there is overwhelming evidence that making an emotional connection is critical to your success as a salesperson. Once you accept that reality, adopt some strategies for making an emotional connection with your potential customers. You want each of them to have a positive, personal feeling about you, your company, and your product or service.

Look for the Right Hook

You can probably think of dozens of words to describe how feelings boil down to a handful of basic emotions. When communicating about your product or service, you obviously don't want to evoke the negative emotions: sadness, disgust, anger, or fear. To connect with your customers, focus on positive emotions like these:

- Joy
- Trust
- Anticipation
- Interest
- Enthusiasm
- Laughter
- Empathy
- Curiosity

Determine which of the positive emotions provides the most obvious emotional hook for your product or service. There may also be limited circumstances in which appealing to a negative emotion (like fear) may be appropriate.

It Doesn't Matter What You're Selling

The authors of *The Experience Economy*, B. Joseph Pine II and James H. Gilmore, assert that your customers want you to engage them "positively, emotionally and memorably." Their views are shared by Tony Hsieh, the CEO of Zappos.com, a $1 billion online e-commerce company that is now part of Amazon.com. Hsieh believes that every call should be treated as an opportunity to make an emotional connection with a customer.

I don't care how boring your product or service is. If you focus on an emotional hook, you will not find it difficult to help your customer connect with it. Here's an example. I purposely chose a product you would not normally associate with emotional content: air conditioners.

Let's assume you are a homeowner in the market for a new air conditioner. You call two reputable companies, and they each send a salesperson to your home. The first salesperson you meet is Bob. The second one is Stan.

Bob promptly hands you a glossy manufacturer's brochure for the product he represents. He discusses its technical specifications, noting its seasonal energy efficiency ratio, the decibel range of the noise it generates, and the benefits of its programmable digital thermostat. He describes the capacity of the unit he is proposing to install for your house. He emphasizes the high quality of the compressor, since that is the most critical component. He tells you that he is eager to make this sale and will give you a 10 percent discount if you place the order before the end of the month.

Now Stan shows up at your home. He begins the meeting by asking questions about your requirements and budget. He listens to your responses and waits for you to ask questions. When you do, he answers in a manner that tells you he understands your concerns. Then he asks more questions, if appropriate. Here's an example of your dialogue:

You: What kind of compressor does this have?

Stan: We use a scroll compressor. That's the gold standard for compressors on air conditioning systems. Are you asking that question because you're concerned about maintenance costs?

You: Yes. That's a big concern of ours.

Stan: Well, you should know that scroll compressors have 70 percent fewer moving parts and a far less complex internal suction and discharge valve, so we can keep your maintenance costs to a minimum.

If you had indicated that your concern was not having to replace the system for many years, Stan would have responded with information about the long-term warranty that comes with this type of compressor.

It's important to note what Stan didn't do. He didn't engage in an initial data dump, extolling the virtues of his product and service. He "ditched the pitch." He didn't promise something he couldn't deliver, like telling you that buying his product would cool the house to such a degree that bugs would flee and you wouldn't need an exterminator. An exaggerated claim would have destroyed his credibility and eliminated the critical element of trust.

Stan didn't discuss how his company got started, its history, how successful it is, the reputation of the air conditioner he represents, or the names of famous people who use his product. Most people don't care. If they do, they will ask.

The Role of Empathy

I discussed the critical role of empathy in Chapter 5. You can't create an emotional connection with your customers unless you fully understand and appreciate their feelings.

When Lou Gerstner became the CEO of IBM in the early 1990s, he sent his top fifty managers to visit five customers each. They were instructed not to sell anything. Their sole goal was to listen, get an understanding of how the customer felt about IBM, and see if there was any way IBM could help them. These visits resulted in IBM gaining a major foothold in e-commerce. IBM also gained insights into how it could better serve its customers. It revamped its customer service in response to the input received at these meetings. This is a good example of how understanding the feelings of your customers can have a major, positive impact on your business.

Making a Reverse Emotional Connection

Sometimes, when the opportunity arises, it is possible to make what I call a "reverse emotional connection." You can do this only if given the right opening by your prospect. Think of it as receiving permission to talk about yourself.

Suppose a customer asks Stan how he got into the air conditioning business. Stan has two basic choices. He can assume the prospect is not really interested in the details of his personal journey. If he goes this route, he will briefly explain that he went to trade school, got a job as an air conditioning apprentice technician, and "the rest is history."

If he wants to make an emotional connection, he can tell the real story. Maybe he lived in a home with no air conditioning and wanted to be sure others could afford it. Perhaps his father and grandfather were in the business and he looked up to them. Maybe he likes to be in a line of work where he makes people happy by increasing the comfort and value of their homes. These reasons all demonstrate why he is so enthused about his job.

However mundane the story may seem, telling the truth in a personal way will give your customer an insight into who you really are and what values you hold dear. It can be a very effective way to make an emotional connection.

An Expensive Lesson

Here's a true story of how I blew the opportunity for a significant sale because I presented data without making an emotional connection. It happened very early in my career as an investment advisor. I received a call from a senior partner at a large accounting firm. He had read one of my books and wanted me to meet with him and his wife to discuss investing his assets. He was contemplating retirement and thought this might be a good time to revisit his investing strategy. He had significant assets. I was eager to meet with him, even though it required traveling to the West Coast.

I met with the prospect and his wife in a quiet corner of a hotel lobby. I was armed with charts, graphs, and long-term risk and return data on the portfolios I thought might be suitable for them. I assumed this data would be of interest because of the man's accounting background. I spent at least thirty minutes presenting all the reasons why my recommendations made sense.

The couple greeted my presentation with little enthusiasm. They asked a few perfunctory questions. They showed very little interest. The meeting ended limply. I never heard back from them. I failed to establish a relationship of trust and confidence.

It was this experience that inspired me to embark on extensive research on how to be effective in sales. I never presented in this manner again.

A Better Way to Present

Now when I meet prospective clients, I always ask them about their goals. Many people have not thought about why they invest. They have very general goals, like "I want to amass as much money as possible." When I get that kind of answer, I ask this question: "Would you consider it a worthy goal to be as certain as you can that you will never run out of money during your life and your partner's life, and will be able to maintain your quality of life and will never be a burden to family and friends?" No one has ever said no to that question.

Then I ask whether they would find it helpful if we could craft a plan that would meet this goal. The answer is always yes. I then gather the information I need to prepare this plan. The data I ultimately present to them is very customized to their specific needs and circumstances. It basically says, "Given these assumptions, if you follow this plan there is only an X percent chance you will run out of money before you or your partner die." If we have made realistic assumptions, the chance of their running out of money is very low.

In my new style of presenting, I use three strategies:

- I ask questions.
- I listen to the responses.
- I directly connect the data I am conveying to a powerful emotion.

Information presented in this way makes a very strong emotional connection. Many of us have a primal fear of being homeless. By connecting with that emotion and offering a plan to combat it, data that would otherwise be mind-numbing becomes riveting.

Doug Fleener, the president of a firm that consults with retailers, provides this example of making an emotional connection in retail sales. Suppose a woman is shopping for an expensive outfit. Instead of asking her what kind of clothes she is looking for, the salesperson asks, "Say it's your birthday, and your friends are going to take you out for dinner and drinks. And you want to look sharp. I mean *really* sharp. I mean look-at-me-world sharp. What type of outfit would you want to wear?" You can almost feel the emotional connection made by this inquiry.

As Fleener notes, someone selling memberships in the American Automobile Association might say, "For one fee, you get emergency roadside assistance." Instead, what if they said, "If you or any member of your family has a breakdown in any area, at any time, help is one call away."

Here's another example based on my personal experience. I met with a sixty-year-old retired businessman in the Midwest. Prior to our meeting, he introduced me to his stunning thirty-something girlfriend. His parents had died. He had no heirs other than his girlfriend, to whom he was leaving his entire fortune. He had sold his business and had enormous wealth. He lived very frugally and was lamenting the fact that he was not enjoying his wealth.

I asked him why he found it so difficult to spend a small portion of his savings. He had trouble giving me a rational explanation. I told him to imagine that he had died and his girlfriend had inherited his money. I asked him to project five years forward from the date of his death and to visualize her life. He thought for several minutes and then said, "She would be married, with children, and they would all be spending my money like they won the lottery." He told me years later that this conversation changed the way he lived his life. I had connected with him in a powerful, emotional way.

It's not difficult to present information in a way that makes an emotional connection.

WHAT'S THE POINT?

Adopting simple strategies for making an emotional connection with your customers will significantly improve your sales.

CHAPTER 9

Don't Assume

A sales strategy based on assumptions is
pure wishful thinking.
—Dave Brock

Assumptions are judgments we make that cause us to believe something is true, even though there is no valid basis for our view. Like many others, salespeople are prone to making assumptions. Often they are incorrect. Many sales have been lost due to incorrect assumptions.

It's Easy to Make Incorrect Assumptions

One day a woman was swimming at her gym. The person in the next lane was obviously agitated. Finally, he yelled at her and (as she later found out) accused her of being rude for not responding to his efforts to talk to her. She explained that she was not being rude. She was deaf.

I had a personal experience with making an assumption that turned out to be laughably wrong. I was trying a case where I represented a large hotel chain. An employee claimed he was discriminated against because of his religion. The trial was held in New York City. The jury consisted of mostly white-collar executives, a few college students, and a burly construction worker who could have been a stunt double for Arnold Schwarzenegger.

During the trial, I felt I was doing well with the executives on the jury, and especially with the college students. They sent subtle, nonverbal signals indicating agreement with the points I was making. The construction worker glared at me throughout the trial.

The jury deliberated for most of the day and delivered its verdict exonerating my client around six that evening. It was midwinter and already dark in New York. It took me a while to gather my papers and head down to the lobby of the federal building, which was mostly deserted by the time I got there. As I started to walk toward the exit of the building, I saw the construction worker walking slowly toward me. He could not have looked more menacing. I looked around for the security guards. Was this it? I saw no escape.

He walked up to me, extended his hand, and said, "You did a great job. I knew the case against the hotel was bulls—t. It took me a while to convince the smart-ass college kids and the big executives, but they finally came around." I was stunned.

That experience taught me two very valuable lessons:

- Don't make assumptions.
- Don't underestimate your audience.

A successful salesperson will never violate these basic principles.

The Perils of Making Assumptions

Assumptions are bad for business. They can create misunderstandings, cause stress, lower your self-confidence, create unnecessary obstacles, and possibly cause you to lose a sale that was yours for the asking.

One common assumption is that you know more about the service or product you are selling than your customer does. As a result, you can quickly slip into "lecture mode."

An investment advisor told me this story: She received an inquiry via phone from a potential client. She explained to him how she focuses on academic data when making investment recommendations. One element of her analysis is to consider the risk of a portfolio. Risk is measured by "standard deviation," a technical term not well understood by the general public. She felt a more comprehensive explanation might be helpful in making the sale.

Her explanation took quite a while. The potential client listened very patiently. When the advisor finally paused, he asked, "Are you done?" She said she was. He then said, "I have a graduate degree from MIT. My major was statistics." The advisor didn't mean to be patronizing. She thought she was being helpful by "educating" the potential client on a basic principle of investing. She made an incorrect assumption. To her credit, she was able to recover, and eventually he agreed to use her as his advisor.

Common Assumptions

Here are some other assumptions commonly made by salespeople:

- The prospective client wants to hear my sales pitch.
- I'm giving the prospective client useful information.

- The information I'm giving is being received in the manner I intend.

- The person I'm meeting has the authority to make the buying decision.

- My product or service meets the perceived need of the customer.

- The price of my product or service is competitive.

- My relationship with the prospective customer is better than it really is.

If any of these examples sound familiar, catch yourself the next time you fall into the "assumption trap." The reality is, we often engage in poor communication with our prospective clients and pass like ships in the night.

The Cure

Fortunately, the cure for making assumptions is simple: Stop. Ask questions. Heed the admonition of President Ronald Reagan: "Trust but verify."

WHAT'S THE POINT?

Successful salespeople avoid making assumptions.

CHAPTER 10

Question

Effective questioning brings insight, which fuels curiosity, which
cultivates wisdom.

—Chip Bell

Your prospective customer has an agenda. She has
needs. She has constraints, like time and budget. You
know nothing about her. You want to help her.

Here's the issue: You also want to make the sale. You
are prepared to present all the reasons the client should buy.
Of course, you will engage in the usual chitchat about the
weather and family, but you are impatiently waiting for the
opportunity to pounce, gauge the reaction, and (hopefully)
achieve your sales goals for the month. I think of most

salespeople as pythons, coiled and waiting to strike. Not a very appealing image, is it?

There's a better way. To become a great salesperson, remember these words: "Ask questions."

Consultative Selling

An entire consulting industry has been built around a sales concept called "consultative selling." This approach, which became prominent in the early 1970s, is the process of eliciting information from your prospective client to determine her needs and then recommending a product or service that meets those needs. When you engage in consultative selling, you shift your focus away from "making the sale" and toward meeting the needs of the customer.

While an in-depth discussion of consultative selling is beyond the scope of this book, the underlying premise is worthy of further discussion. By asking questions and listening carefully to the responses, you can get a full and complete understanding of the needs of your customer. In many cases, understanding those needs will result in a sale. When it doesn't, you will still be providing value by directing your client elsewhere or giving other advice based on the response you received to your questions.

Tips for Asking Questions

Asking the right questions, at the right time, requires study, skill, and experience. Here are some tips:

Keep your goals in mind. According to marketing expert Erica Stritch, asking questions can help you to:

- Build rapport and a relationship based on trust
- Uncover the aspirations and goals of your customer
- Make the impact of what you are providing clear and powerful
- Provide a solution to the problems expressed by the client

The questions you ask should advance these goals.

Plan your questions. Some questions flow naturally from the conversation. For example, if you were a pharmaceutical representative and a doctor told you, "My patients have experienced a lot of side effects with that drug," it would be only natural to ask follow-up questions in order to obtain a more complete understanding of the issue.

Nevertheless, you should always spend some time in advance preparing key questions you believe will help you understand the needs of your prospective customer. When I get an inquiry about a speaking engagement, I ask the person to tell me something about their group. I also ask about positive and negative experiences they have had with other speakers. The responses help me connect with my audience and craft a better presentation.

Don't read questions from a script. I am amazed by how many people feel they need to rely on something written for even the simplest interaction. I have seen lawyers give opening statements to juries by reading from a large yellow pad: "My name is John Smith and it is my privilege to represent the plaintiff in this action, Bill Jones." Surely they can remember their own name and who they represent!

Nothing impedes effective communication more than not making eye contact and appearing rehearsed. Take time to memorize the two or three main areas of inquiry you need to explore at the meeting. Ask your questions in a normal conversational tone.

Don't ask loaded questions. Never underestimate the intelligence of your prospective customers. They know when they are being manipulated. Questions like "Why do you believe we might be the right fit for your company?" should never be asked. Your goal is to genuinely determine their needs. Don't assume that their needs and your product or service are a good fit.

Don't cross-examine. Effective questioning should not feel like an invasion of privacy or an inquisition. Ask only those questions that are necessary to fully understand the needs of the client. If you really need personal information, ask for permission first. To avoid inundating the client with too many questions, you may want to schedule a series of meetings. Don't feel you have to learn everything in the first meeting.

Ask open-ended questions. Questions that start with "What," "Why," or "How" encourage longer, more discursive answers. You want to encourage your prospective customer to open up and convey as much information as possible.

Cede control. The right question can transfer control from you to the prospective client—where it belongs. Here's an example: "What would you like me to do as the next step?" This is far better than saying, "I will follow up with you next week to see where you are with the decision-making process."

Ditch the pitch. Hard pitches may work well in baseball, but not in sales. They cause people to recoil, act defensively, and become suspicious and resistant. You can't ask questions when you are "lecturing."

An Example of Consultative Selling

Eric Baron and David Hauer of the Baron Group provide this example of how consultative selling has impacted the way pharmaceutical representatives market drugs to busy physicians. These reps need to capitalize on the precious few moments allotted by the doctor. The old way was to give a frenzied pitch about the merits of the drugs *du jour*, leave a bunch of samples, and depart.

The new process breaks the selling cycle into these recommended phases:

Phase 1: A brief introductory meeting. The representative explains that he wants to spend more time at the next meeting to get to know the needs of the doctor better.

Phase 2: At the second meeting, the representative asks questions about the needs, concerns, and issues on the mind of the doctor.

Phase 3: At the third meeting, the representative presents options from which the doctor can make an intelligent choice.

By using this consultative approach, the representative has gone from a supplier of samples to a problem solver who is genuinely interested in serving the best interest of his client.

Trust Trumps Everything

Of all the goals of consultative selling, the most important one is building a rapport based on trust and confidence. If you are able to achieve this goal, you may find that nothing more is required.

I recently had a personal experience that illustrates this point. I have taken some literary license to protect the confidentiality of the client.

I was asked by a reader of my books to meet with him at his office in the Midwest to discuss his investments. He was a very successful, retired real estate developer and philanthropist with a huge amount of assets. He explained that he was interviewing a number of investment advisors and didn't want me to make the trip to his office unless I understood that he was engaging in extensive due diligence. I told him that was fine with me and I looked forward to the meeting.

We met at his office. He was sitting behind a large desk. He told me he had only one hour to devote to this meeting. I decided not to focus initially on questions I had prepared that related to investing. Instead, I opened the meeting with this inquiry: "Tell me how you got to where you are today." It turns out that he had a very interesting Horatio Alger story. His success was due to hard work and incredible perseverance, coupled with excellent timing. He sold his vast real estate holdings prior to the 2008 housing crash. He and his wife devoted much of their time to their charitable foundation.

His response to my opening question led very naturally to more questions. Why did he retire? What does he plan to do with the rest of his life? What drew him to philanthropy? How does he select the charities he supports? How many children and grandchildren does he have? What is his view on leaving a large inheritance to them? What is the legacy he wants to leave?

The answers to these questions took more than our allotted hour. We never discussed my firm, the risk and return data of our portfolios, my views on investing, or anything else related to the services we provide or how I function as an advisor. It was a very enjoyable conversation for me. I have a genuine interest in other people and want to learn what is important to them.

As I started to ask another question, he interrupted me and said something that took me by surprise: "I really enjoyed meeting you and want to retain you as my advisor. You are the fourth person I've interviewed and I have two more scheduled, but I'm going to cancel those appointments. I am very comfortable with you. I feel like you understand me and will do a great job for me." I thanked him and went on my way.

We had built a rapport. He trusted me. He didn't need to know anything more. Presumably, he had already done due diligence by reading my books and researching my firm. He wanted to entrust his fortune to someone he liked and respected. Once that threshold was reached, he felt no need to review data and charts.

I am not suggesting that every meeting will go as well as this one. But you can increase your odds once you shift from thinking it is all about you and your presentation to an intense focus on your prospective customer. You can't understand her needs without asking questions and listening very carefully to the responses. I discuss developing your listening skills in the next chapter.

WHAT'S THE POINT?

Asking the right questions will materially increase your ability to close sales.

CHAPTER 11

Listen

When people talk, listen completely.
Most people never listen.
—Ernest Hemingway

Martha and Jay Braintree are a fictional couple, but the story that follows is representative of clients with whom I have worked. You may recognize this scenario from your own experience.

Martha, age sixty-seven, returned home from a busy day of shopping. Her husband, Jay, age seventy, was retired from his job as the owner of a small electrical contracting firm in Lenox, Massachusetts. They had been happily married for almost forty years.

Martha saw Jay's truck and knew he would be at home, waiting for her. She rang the doorbell because her arms were full of groceries. No one answered. She unlocked the door and entered the house. She will never forget the scene that confronted her.

Jay was lying on the floor of the foyer. He was motionless. Martha dropped her grocery bags. "Jay!" she yelled. "Jay, what happened?" No response. She turned him over, which was not an easy task. His eyes opened and he struggled to speak. His voice was a soft whisper and his words were slurred.

Martha grabbed her cell phone and frantically dialed 911. "Send an ambulance. Something is terribly wrong with my husband. He's lying on the floor of the foyer." The emergency operator asked a series of questions: "What happened? Is he conscious? Did he fall? Can he speak?" All Martha knew was that Jay was conscious and trying to speak. She told the operator she needed to tend to him. She was told an ambulance was being immediately dispatched and would arrive within minutes.

"Jay," she said, "can you tell me what happened?" All she could make out were these words: "Fell. Help me." "It's okay, honey," she said. "The ambulance is coming.

You're going to be fine. Don't worry. I'll take care of you and will never leave you." She heard the siren of the approaching ambulance. "They're almost here, honey," she said. Jay was trying to say something. She thought it was "I love you," but she wasn't sure.

Several things about this story are meaningful to you. In order to help Jay, Martha knew she had to elicit information. She did so by asking questions. She didn't interrupt him. Once she had the information, she used it to maximize his chances for recovery. The level of her listening was intense. She was totally focused on trying to understand him and getting him the help he needed as quickly as possible. Her only agenda was devotion to his best interest and extreme empathy with his condition.

That's the level of listening you want to have in your conversations with prospective customers.

Listening Isn't Always Easy

Good listening is surprisingly difficult. This is especially true for salespeople. We have an agenda. We have a product or service. We want to make a sale. Many salespeople regard any conversation not directly related to whatever it is they are selling as wasteful, distracting, and even annoying.

Men are particularly vulnerable to this way of thinking. I remember many years ago when I was in desperate need of a new pair of shoes. My wife offered to go shopping with me. Shopping is something I really do not enjoy. We were in a large department store, en route to the shoe department. As we were passing the men's sportswear area, my wife pointed to some sports jackets and asked me if I wanted to try them on. I responded, "We came to buy shoes and that's all I want to do." Men are the traditional hunters. We seek our prey. We don't want to be distracted.

I later realized how silly I had been. We were already in the store. What difference would it make if I took ten minutes and tried on a couple of sports jackets? My wife was trying to tell me that my casual wardrobe was pretty well worn and needed an update. I wasn't listening.

Competitive versus Genuine Listening

Picture this scenario: You are a stockbroker. An elderly widow comes in to see you. She has inherited five million dollars. She doesn't know how to invest it. She is very unsophisticated, but she has some general ideas of her investment goals, which she explains to you as best she can.

Are you really listening to this potential client? Or are you are figuring out what you can sell to maximize your commission? The latter is "competitive" listening. You are pretending to have a genuine interest in *her* agenda, while your mind is focused on *your* needs.

If you were engaged in genuine listening (sometimes called "reflective" listening), here's how you would be interacting with the widow: "I understand your primary concern is making sure you don't run out of money during your lifetime, but you would also like to leave an inheritance to your children. Do I have that right?"

By genuinely listening to her answers to these questions, you would gain enough information to provide your prospective client with the best investment solution for her, even though it might be inconsistent with your self-interest.

Listening Tips

So how can you become better at listening? Here are some suggestions to keep in mind.

Avoid selective listening. Training yourself to become a genuine, reflective listener will require dedicated effort to reverse your default behavior. The way you listen may be affected by what is being said. Here are three examples:

Scenario 1: You are attending a lecture in introductory chemistry. The lecturer is discussing properties of gases, including the kinetic molecular theory. You are bored and confused. You can't help being distracted.

Scenario 2: Your best friend's father died. She is understandably distraught and has called to discuss her grief. You listen intently. You care about her and want to do your best to comfort her.

Scenario 3: You are at a party and meet a new person. He launches into a dialogue about the current presidential race, the relative merits of the candidates, and his strongly held views about several key issues. While he is speaking, you are thinking about all the points you are going to make to show him how his political and personal opinions are clearly wrong.

It's easy to identify Scenario 2 as an opportunity for genuine listening. But ideally, you should be listening intently in all three scenarios. If your goal is to get a high mark in your chemistry class, you should pay attention to everything that is being said. If you care about your friend, you will want to give her the opportunity to fully express her feelings without interrupting. If you are open to new relationships, you will want to listen carefully to the views of your new social acquaintance, even though you may not agree with them or might not be interested in them.

If you "tune out" in some situations, you're being a selective listener. Selective listening can be very harmful to your ability to make a sale. If you engage in selective listening based on your interests and biases, you may fail to recognize the value your prospective client is placing on subjects you are excluding. If you react negatively (and instantly) to something that is being said, you may be making the incorrect assumption that you are being asked for your opinion, when in reality the other person may just want to be heard.

Stop talking. I know it's obvious, but you can't listen and talk at the same time. To gauge whether you are predominately listening or talking, apply the "80/20 rule." Listen 80 percent of the time. Talk only 20 percent of the time. I have had thousands of interactions with salespeople over the years. None of them has come close to applying this rule. I have to work really hard to comply with it myself. Our normal inclination is to believe that what we are saying is very important and everyone is interested in it.

There is a massive disconnect between our perception of ourselves as effective listeners and reality. In one study of more than eight hundred business people, virtually all those surveyed thought they were great listeners. More objective studies have found that the average person has a listening efficiency rate of a meager 25 percent.

There is a serious payoff if you can suppress your normal inclination to talk. How do you want your customers to perceive you? Is being thought of as glib, slick, or someone who has all the answers really the impression you want to create?

In stark contrast, think about these perceptions: "Really understood what I was trying to convey." "Thoughtful." "Analytical." If the prospective client called her spouse and described you in those terms, wouldn't you feel like you had made a terrific impression? It's no guarantee you will make the sale, but you will have definitely skewed the odds in your favor.

Let the prospect speak first. Salespeople often assume they should "go first" and begin the conversation with a lengthy monologue. This is a critical error. Give the other person permission to talk freely by asking a short, appropriate, open-ended question. Here's one suggested by a site devoted to marketing for travel agents: "Tell me about your all-time favorite trip and what made it memorable."

Avoid interrupting. The opposite of listening is interrupting. Interrupting sends all the wrong messages. It can be perceived as rude. It conveys a lack of interest in what is being said. It shows a lack of respect for the speaker. You can learn a lot from police detectives doing an interrogation of a suspect. They are taught to ask a question and then to refrain from doing anything that might cause the suspect to stop talking.

Most of us are not aware of our tendency to interrupt. Try this exercise. Ask your family or friends, "Do I interrupt you when you're speaking to me?" You may be surprised at the response. If it is "yes," ask them to make it a point to tell you every time you interrupt them, regardless of the context. Also keep a mental scorecard of the times you interrupt others. You will be amazed at how often you fall into this trap. Remember, the key to effective selling is eliciting information and listening to what is being said. What you are saying is of far less importance.

Be patient. Even when what is being said is clearly wrong or offensive, let the other person completely finish the thought. Follow up with questions instead of statements.

Pause before replying. When your potential customer stops talking, you may think you need to respond instantly, but you don't. Pausing for a few seconds before replying insures that your potential customer has stopped speaking. It also gives you the opportunity to carefully consider what was said instead of responding with a canned script.

Paraphrase. It is important for your customer to be confident that you understand her views. You can achieve this goal by paraphrasing back what was conveyed to you. If you're a jeweler and a young man is discussing his requirements for an engagement ring, you might paraphrase his comments like this: "So, I understand you don't want to spend more than twenty-five hundred dollars, you want a heart-shaped diamond, and you want a certificate listing the characteristics of your diamond. Did I understand you correctly?"

Don't assume you're being asked for advice. I have fallen into the "giving advice" trap more times than I can count. Given my background as a lawyer and an investment advisor, it's easy for me to assume prospective clients want my advice. This is rarely the case. Most people know what they want. They may just want you to acknowledge that you are hearing their views.

Here's an example. You are in the business of selling used cars. Your customer tells you all the bad experiences she has had with used car salesmen. Instead of assuming she wants your advice about which used car to purchase, you simply state, "I understand your past experiences with used car salespeople have been very bad. I know you must be concerned about not repeating that experience with me."

There is a big difference between listening and giving advice. Most parents of children in their teens or twenties (or beyond) have learned this the hard way. Frequently, our children just want to feel like we hear them. They find it offensive if we offer solutions when we are not specifically asked to do so (and sometimes, even if we are!).

Dr. Scott Williams, who teaches business management at Wright State University, provides this example based on his personal experience. In response to the typical inquiry from a colleague asking, "How are things going?" he confided that he was wrestling with a difficult problem. The response of his colleague was to tell him how to solve the problem.

Dr. Williams noted, "That really bothered me. I value self-reliance and I like solving puzzles, so I don't like someone telling me how to solve my problems. . . If he would have just listened instead of advising, I would have shared more and we would have built a stronger bond."

I am not suggesting that your prospective client will never want your advice. After you have elicited information from her and carefully listened to it, there will come a time when the client asks you questions. This is the time to provide advice, geared specifically to what is on the client's mind.

Be careful to not interrupt women. There is considerable evidence that women are interrupted more than men. Both genders are guilty of engaging in this activity. Be particularly sensitive about interrupting a woman. She will appreciate it.

Harness the power of rapt attention. Flattery, when done in a manipulative way, is a very poor sales strategy. People aren't stupid. They understand when they are being played. But according to Dale Carnegie, the author of the iconic book *How to Win Friends and Influence People*, "Rapt attention is the highest form of flattery." Think about that for a moment. By simply listening intently to what your sales prospect is telling you, you demonstrate genuine interest and concern.

WHAT'S THE POINT?

Genuine, intense listening is an important sales strategy.

CHAPTER 12

Connect with Both Men and Women

Men are from Earth, women are from Earth. Deal with it.
—George Carlin

If you have a "one size fits all" approach to sales, you are making a critical mistake. The same presentation will be processed very differently by the brains of the men and women who are hearing it. Understanding these differences is critical to your success in selling to both genders.

The Oxytocin Difference in Men and Women

The brains of men and women are impacted by a hormone

called oxytocin. This brain chemical has the effect of reducing stress and promoting social bonding. Although men and women have similar levels of this hormone, the fact that women have higher levels of estrogen may be the reason they are more favorably impacted by oxytocin. The relationship between estrogen and oxytocin is thought to explain why women are less aggressive than men and have what is termed a "tend-and-befriend" response to social situations.

Unfortunately for men, the male sex hormone (testosterone) can act to *reduce* the level of oxytocin. It can also increase the level of another hormone called vasopressin, which has been shown to *enhance* aggression.

These hormonal differences may account for the aggressive response by men to stressful situations, compared to the calmer, "tend-and-befriend" reaction of women. It may also be the reason why women are more comfortable sharing their feelings, which causes their oxytocin levels to rise.

Communication Differences Between the Genders

Given our hormonal dissimilarities, it's not surprising that men and women communicate differently. One study found that the conversation of women is more personal and more focused. Women tend to interrupt far less frequently than men. They encourage participation by everyone. Men avoid discussing their personal feelings, discuss many topics, and seek to dominate the conversation. They do so to establish hierarchy. They want to be the "alpha dog."

The focus of men on dominance and women on feelings, and the ensuing difficulty in making an emotional connection, has been well documented. If you are a man selling to a woman, you need to be aware that you are innately wired to use conversation as a vehicle for "educating" her. She, on the other hand, may be using the conversation as a way to establish a relationship with you. While these goals are not necessarily mutually exclusive, unless you are aware of them, you will pass like ships in the night. You can't communicate with someone you don't understand.

Communicating with Women

No one solution is right for all interactions between genders. But common sense tells you that a man selling to a woman would be wise to mirror her behavior as much as possible and to avoid stereotypical conduct associated with male communication patterns. A woman looking for an emotional connection is not going to find it with a man who talks louder, lectures to her, interrupts her, and generally attempts to dominate the conversation in order to establish his alpha male credentials.

A more effective strategy would be to make inquiries that will elicit her views on exactly what she needs and wants from you. Repeat back what she has said so she knows you understood her. Don't interrupt, even if you feel compelled to do so. She needs to understand that she can trust you to act in her best interest and that your goal is not just to make a sale. Women selling to another woman should follow the same guidelines.

The potential for salespersons (of both genders) who understand how to sell to women is huge. According to Cynthia Tidwell, an expert on leadership, women's health, and financial security, women influence over 80 percent of all consumer purchases and spend about $5 trillion annually. They also are big referrers. A woman will refer up to twenty-eight friends and acquaintances to a trustworthy vendor. A man refers an average of only thirteen.

Communicating with Men

What if you are a man or woman attempting to make a sale to a man? Here's a simple strategy: Make his weaknesses your strengths. You know he wants to dominate the conversation. Let him. He wants to speak louder than you. Fine. He wants to show he knows more about your product or service than you do. No problem. Demonstrate your genuine interest in what he is saying by your body language. Lean forward. Maintain eye contact with him. Ask questions. The more he talks, the more likely your sales efforts will be successful. You are not there to compete with him. There is room for only one alpha male in a conversation. You want that role to be his.

WHAT'S THE POINT?

By understanding the differences in how men and women communicate, you increase your ability to sell to them.

CHAPTER 13

Limit Use of PowerPoint

I would go so far as to say that almost all business presentations given with PowerPoint, with a little extra work, would be better—even much better—without it.
—Steven H. Kaminski

Technology that permits us to deliver even more data can be counterproductive. The most widely used presentation tool is PowerPoint. A whiteboard (which permits nonpermanent markings on a glossy surface) is a close second. In limited circumstances, both tools can be effective in large group settings. In smaller meetings—and particularly in one-on-one presentations—they can be a barrier to effective communication and an obstacle to establishing an emotional connection.

Issues with PowerPoint in Smaller Meetings

You can find thousands of books and articles about improving your PowerPoint presentations. I suggest you ignore all of them and adopt this rule instead: *never use PowerPoint in a one-on-one presentation or a small group setting.* Putting up a wall between you and your customer is the worst possible way to make a sales presentation. In fact, the term "sales presentation" is a misnomer. You don't want to "present" anything. You want to listen, understand, and respond to the needs of your audience.

In his book *Presentation Zen: Simple Ideas on Presentation Design and Delivery*, Garr Reynolds correctly observes that overwhelming your audience with data can be the kiss of death. Instead, he notes the importance of making an emotional connection with your audience and using some humor or "play."

What's the first thing you think of when someone stands up and launches into a presentation of vast amounts of information? It probably reminds you of your experiences in school. You sat quietly while the instructors lectured you. Often there was little or no interaction. They talked. You listened.

It is not easy to establish an emotional connection with your potential customer. The use of PowerPoint can make it more difficult. It permits you to overwhelm your customer with data she will not retain, potentially boring her. And it inhibits genuine listening on your part, since you will be doing all the talking.

When PowerPoint *May* Be Effective

There are limited scenarios when PowerPoint may have a role in presentations to larger groups. If you want to share information that could be more easily summarized using graphs and charts, or if a picture would convey your message more effectively, you should consider the use of PowerPoint. There is considerable research showing that visuals are processed sixty thousand times faster than text.

The right visuals can help create an emotional connection with a large audience. Mike Parkinson, a visual communication expert, provides these examples. A picture of a joyous baby evokes feelings and emotions no text could simulate. A picture of a snarling dog instills fear in a nanosecond. Parkinson notes that our brains decipher images instantaneously. Text is decoded in a sequential manner, at a much slower rate.

PowerPoint Tips

If you're in a situation where PowerPoint may be an effective tool, here's how to use it to best advantage.

Use a professional designer. If you are speaking to a large group, you are making an important presentation. Using standard templates dilutes your impact. A professional designer will use higher quality photography and more engaging layouts. Professionals also understand the impact of different colors and patterns. The overall design will be far superior to anything you could do on your own.

Make your presentation fun and playful. A director friend once told me, "First you entertain and then you educate." There's wisdom in those words. If audience members are bored, they are not going to pay attention to anything you present. Think out-of-the-box. Inject humor in your slides when possible. In one presentation about investing that I made to a large group, I used cartoon-like characters in my slides to illustrate my points. It was very effective.

On the other hand, don't get carried away with your comedic efforts. You are most likely not a professional comedian. You don't want to come across as trying too hard to be something you aren't. You also don't want to distract your audience from your core message. Be sure that your humor will not offend anyone in your audience.

Limit text. How many times have you attended a PowerPoint presentation where each slide was filled with a list of bullet points? Depending on where you were sitting, it may have been impossible to read the text. If the text is the same as what the speaker is saying, what's the point of repeating it on the slide? Putting too much text on PowerPoint slides is the most common misuse of the software. Your slides should be primarily graphics, with as little text as possible. The best presentations I have attended had no text on the slides at all.

Focus. Your PowerPoint presentation should reinforce your focal points. For example, if you are discussing how to get a book published, your focal points could be:

- Come up with an idea for a book.
- Write a book proposal.
- Get a literary agent.

Within each point, you would make a number of observations, but you want the audience focused on this basic outline. PowerPoint can be effective in maintaining your focus.

Issues with Whiteboards

What about the use of the manual whiteboard in small settings? It suffers from the same problems as PowerPoint:

- It encourages speaking instead of listening.
- It encourages conveying significant amounts of data that can be difficult to process.
- It discourages communicating feelings and emotions.
- It encourages one-way communication, which practically assures miscommunication and lack of understanding.
- It's boring, because the listener has to wait for you to write on the whiteboard.

Have you ever seen a presenter go to the whiteboard and write something really obvious on it, like "I will be making five important points today"? While she is doing that, what are you thinking? If you're like me, your thoughts range from "This is going to be long and boring" to "I can't believe she feels the need to actually write that down. Does she think I'm an idiot?" Are these the impressions you want your prospective customer to have about you?

Follow the Lead of the Professionals

When you are crafting a presentation to any size audience, you might find it helpful to emulate the techniques of professional speakers. I have attended many talks by riveting speakers. Most of them were sales-related. None of the speakers used any visual aids. They all told stories, both about themselves and about others. They wanted the audience to get to know them as people and to understand their motivations. They all had a passion for their message. They used storytelling to convey their points. They didn't hide behind bullet points of text on slides. They made an emotional connection with their audience. You can learn a lot from them.

WHAT'S THE POINT?

The use of PowerPoint and whiteboards in a small group setting is a sales killer.

CHAPTER 14

E-Connect

Many sites have no photos of warm, happy people or warm scenes anywhere. Hellooooo? Does anyone live here? Who are these people anyhow? Man, this place is cold!
—Matthew Ledford

"Sales" is no longer confined to in-person meetings. Often there is limited or even no personal contact between buyer and seller. Online sales in the United States alone were $155 billion in 2011, up 16.1 percent from 2010, based on estimates issued by the US Commerce Department. These sales account for 4.6 percent of all retail sales in the United States. The US Online Retail Forecast estimates continued growth in online sales from 167 million consumers in 2011 to 192 million in 2016. Total consumer e-retail spending is expected to reach $377 billion in 2016, which would be a 62 percent increase.

"E-commerce" encompasses buying and selling goods and services using the Internet. Perhaps the best examples are Amazon.com, Netflix, and eBay. These companies sell exclusively over the Internet. E-commerce can also refer to companies that use the Internet as an adjunct to their brick-and-mortar stores. Almost every major retail company uses e-commerce in this manner. Prominent examples are Apple, Staples, Walmart, and Best Buy. E-commerce also has a variety of other applications, including business-to-business and business-to-government sales.

Starting an e-commerce site is now possible for almost everyone. The availability of e-commerce hosting companies at a modest cost, and payment options like PayPal, has spurred a growth of small entrepreneurs attempting to cash in on the e-commerce boom. E-commerce site providers like Volusion will build and even manage an online store, providing access to features previously available only to large corporations.

Although e-commerce does not involve personal meetings, the core need to establish an emotional connection with your prospective customer remains the same. Achieving this goal requires a change in strategy. Here are some helpful tips.

Cultivate Trust

The purpose of most websites seems to be to inundate the viewer with a wealth of information. That's the wrong approach. The true goal of your website should be to establish you and your company as reliable, credible, honest, and trustworthy.

How can you gain people's trust online? As a general rule, sites that are perceived as a resource will be deemed more trustworthy than those that only provide information about your products and services. If you are a plastic surgeon, writing blogs about the latest advances in your field of expertise, with hyperlinks to medical journals, would be an example of using your web page as a resource.

Another way to help establish trustworthiness is by indicating that you respect the information users provide and never share it with anyone. Trade awards and testimonials from customers are also helpful in showing that you are honest and reliable.

One study identified these factors as producing a sense of trustworthiness in a website:

- Seals of approval from well-known sites like VeriSign and Visa
- Ease of navigation
- Clear discussion of how orders will be filled
- Clearly defined recourse for returning orders and solving problems
- Site design and presentation that create an overall feeling of quality, professionalism, and advanced technology

Show Your Human Side

I was recently asked to assist a personal trainer who was starting a new business. She is a young, energetic woman with a degree in exercise physiology. She asked me to discuss her website with her. She wanted to highlight her education and her extensive experience as a trainer.

You might guess that I began by asking about her qualifications, but I didn't. Instead, I asked her to show me pictures of her and her family. She proudly took out a bound volume she had created. Inside were dozens of photos of her holding a newborn—her sister's son Billy—

and looking lovingly into his eyes. It would be clear to anyone seeing those pictures that she loves that child. Here's what I told her: "Your biggest business generator is your nephew Billy." She was stunned. How could this be?

The photographs of her and Billy made a powerful impact on me, and I was confident others viewing her website would react the same way. They show a warm, loving, and compassionate person, filled with human kindness. I recommended including one of the pictures of her and Billy on her website, as well as photos of her with her sisters and other family members. These photos will create a powerful emotional connection before she even meets her potential clients.

Regardless of your business, customers are human. They will be more inclined to deal with you if you are a decent, kind, and caring person. You want them to be able to relate to you on a personal, human level. Once those traits are established, you will find a far more receptive audience.

Don't Rely on Slogans

The same personal trainer asked me to evaluate her business cards. They had a black background, with her name, degree, and contact details and the slogan "Feel healthy, stay young." She was thinking of using the same slogan on her website.

I don't like slogans. They sound preachy. If they must be used (which is rarely the case), they should be 100 percent accurate. Training will not keep you "young." You will get older, but training may improve the quality of your life.

I suggested the trainer dump her business cards and redesign them. I encouraged her to lighten the background, lose the slogan, and add a picture of herself. The same advice applies to a website or any other marketing medium. Present yourself as a human being, not a slick slogan.

Use Photos and Video

It's no coincidence that the examples I've shared involve the use of photos. A picture really is worth a thousand words.

I was asked by a boutique law firm to critique their website. They wanted to use it as a marketing tool. It looked like it was done from a standard template. The small photos of formally dressed lawyers showed how serious they were.

I asked the managing partner what he did when he wasn't working. He had a passion for golf. I recommended he post pictures of himself on the golf course and that other partners post pictures of themselves with their families or engaging in activities they enjoy. One member of the law firm had climbed the highest mountain on every continent. I recommended a montage of his experiences, narrated by him. We all admire extraordinary achievement. It acts as an inducement to reach out to that person and learn more about him.

Video can be very effective, but only when it is professionally produced, directed, and shot. The standard video showing you extolling the virtues of your product or service is a waste of your money.

For the personal trainer's website, I suggested adding videos that showed her interacting with clients during training sessions. Those videos convey not just her skill as a trainer, but her keen sense of humor and encouraging, nonthreatening style of training.

A wonderful video that makes a powerful emotional connection was produced to promote the social networking site Google+. The video is narrated by a father who talks about the experience of being a new dad. He took pictures on his cell phone of every aspect of his baby's life. Unfortunately, he lost the phone. What saved the day? All of the pictures were stored on Google+. I challenge you not to be moved by this brief video. Ask yourself how much more powerful it is than a list of the features and benefits of using Google+.

Tell Stories

From a very early age, we are conditioned to like stories. Yet few websites actually tell one. If you sell sneakers, consider telling a story about how you were able to start an exercise program by progressively increasing the distance you walked every day, using your sneakers. If you sell a prescription medication, tell a story about how using it enhanced someone's quality of life. The more personal the better. We can relate to stories. It's hard to feel compassion for facts unconnected to people.

Use Humor and Whimsy

The traits that make people appealing also add luster to websites. Take a look at MailChimp.com, a site for managing email newsletters. It's not just easy to navigate, it's friendly and funny. You can almost feel a personal relationship with someone at this site. Just the image of the cartoon chimp brings a smile to your face. You don't have to be stuffy and serious to attract customers.

Use Videoconferencing

Websites aren't the only way to connect over the Internet. Videoconferencing technology has changed at a rapid rate. It's inexpensive and very user-friendly.

Skype is the granddaddy of videoconferencing services. It was created in 2003 as a way to place free calls over the Internet. In 2006 it expanded its services to videoconferencing. Skype has regularly enhanced its service. The current quality of its videoconferencing is vastly improved.

The newest offerings, like iMeet (iMeet.com), are extremely simple to use. They require no hardware or software. According to Sean O'Brien, an executive for the company behind iMeet, the formula for successful interaction is simple: "The more personal the meeting, the more productive it is." In order to facilitate making a personal connection, iMeet is fully integrated with social media. It lets users upload profile pictures and create a short biography, making it easy for everyone on the video call to quickly find out information about the other participants.

It's impractical and expensive to meet every prospect in person. By adopting videoconferencing technology, you can help bridge the gap by permitting clients to "meet" you via the Internet. This kind of connection is far more effective than using the telephone or communicating by e-mail.

Learn from Iconic Brands

You can learn a lot about making an emotional connection online from the experience of iconic brands. Their advertising agencies need to motivate customers to buy a product. That's precisely the issue that confronts you, whether you are a corporation with a major web presence or an entrepreneur with limited resources.

Milton Pedraza, the chief executive of the Luxury Institute, which studies the buying habits of the rich and famous, attributed the success of famous fragrances like

Chanel No. 5 to "a great fragrance, a great package *and a great emotional theme*" (italics mine).

Coco Chanel was far ahead of her time in recognizing the power of connecting a product to the emotions of her customers. The initial advertising for Chanel No. 5 said nothing about ingredients. Instead, Marilyn Monroe (who wore the fragrance) was featured as saying, "All I wear to bed is a few drops of Chanel No. 5." Enough said!

Making an emotional connection is not limited to luxury goods. I recently viewed a commercial for Dell laptops. Computers are obviously very technical. Typical specifications include processor speed, memory, network cards, storage, and bundled software. What did this expensively produced commercial say about those important specifications? Absolutely nothing.

Instead, it portrayed a happy family of four, including twin sons, who were very close and about to head off to separate colleges. The laptop was used to illustrate how the family would be able to stay in touch using videoconferencing. The commercial evoked powerful feelings of sadness that this family was going to experience a massive change in their lives, followed by happiness at knowing that, thanks to their Dell computer, it would be almost like they were still together.

Apple is the master at creating an emotional bond. Commercials for the iPhone show a boyfriend and girlfriend as they wave to each other using the phone's FaceTime video calling technology. It turns out the boyfriend is deaf, so the couple sign to each other over FaceTime. Millions of people who viewed this commercial were deeply touched.

Another Apple commercial shows a pregnant woman whose husband is deployed in the military. The woman is getting an ultrasound. She shows the picture of the baby on the monitor to her husband. It doesn't show him crying, but I suspect many of those who viewed this brilliant commercial did. I admit to being one of them.

Nike has done what many thought was impossible. It elevated the lowly sneaker to a product associated with courage, empowerment, and pride. The results have been stunning. Nike's revenues exceed $6 billion.

These brands understand a basic principle that should be a guide for everyone engaged in sales, both in person and through e-commerce. Messages that make an emotional connection are far more effective than those that don't. Numerous studies validate this view.

WHAT'S THE POINT?

It is just as important to make an emotional connection online as it is in person.

PART THREE

The Critical Role of Happiness

CHAPTER 15

The Happiness-Success Relationship

Some cause happiness wherever they go;
others whenever they go.
—Oscar Wilde

There's a chicken-and-egg problem when discussing happiness and success. It's easy to assume success will make you happy. This makes sense. If you are struggling financially, you imagine that if you no longer had to worry about money, your life would be easier and more enjoyable. Achieving success in this competitive global economy, and especially during these difficult economic times, is a tall mountain to climb. Once you reach the summit, you might think happiness would inevitably follow.

Unfortunately, this is not the case. Shift your focus from achieving financial success to improving your happiness. In doing so, you are likely to become far more successful in sales.

Financial Success Alone May Not Make You Happy

I'm sure you've heard the refrain "If only I could win the lottery." The implication is that a large infusion of wealth would bring happiness. The data are to the contrary. Statistics show that just slightly more than half of lottery winners are happier than they were before. The "big score" had no effect on more than a third of the winners. A large percentage of the winners (44 percent) spent their entire winnings within five years.

Considerable research indicates that those who focus entirely on achieving financial success have a lower sense of self-worth and more health issues than those who place a premium on activities that give them pleasure or develop a skill.

Nobel laureate Daniel Kahneman does not believe high income makes you happier. In a report of a study he coauthored, Kahneman explains that many people believe high income correlates directly with good moods, satisfaction with their lives, and other aspects of happiness. However, he and his coauthors found that these beliefs are "largely illusory." People with higher incomes are not happier from moment to moment than those with lower incomes. In fact, they are more tense and do not engage in enjoyable activities. The study found that the effect of income on life satisfaction is "transient."

An article by Jennifer Aaker at Stanford University summarized these additional reasons why simply earning more may not make us any happier:

- Higher income earners, on average, don't spend time on things that make them happier. In fact, they seem to spend more time working to buy more "stuff," which creates more stress.

- Most people are never satisfied with what they have. They seem to have an insatiable appetite for more, leading to frustration and stress.

- Once people have met their basic needs, there is little evidence that more income provides more satisfaction or happiness.
- The best predictor of human happiness is successful relationships, especially with family and friends.

I am not suggesting that financial success is irrelevant to your level of happiness. Research indicates that day-to-day happiness continues to increase until annual household income reaches $75,000. That seems to be the amount of income necessary to remove basic economic stress for those living in the United States. Once that income goal is reached, daily happiness plateaus.

Happiness Breeds Success

Although success does not necessarily lead to greater happiness, the reverse seems to be true. Happy people are more likely to be successful.

One exhaustive study reviewed 225 studies on happiness and success. The authors found that happy people are much more likely to have "fulfilling marriages and relationships, high incomes, superior work performance, community involvement, robust health and even a long life." They concluded that happy people are generally more successful across many areas.

The reason for this outcome is that happy people have positive emotions. Their positive attitude permits them to work toward goals and makes it more likely they will achieve them. The lead researcher, Sonja Lyubomirsky, PhD, observed, "When people feel happy, they tend to feel confident, optimistic, and energetic and others find them likable and sociable. Happy people are thus able to benefit from these perceptions."

As you will see, the core traits of successful salespeople are remarkably similar to those of people who lead happy lives. Simply making more money will probably not make you any happier. But implementing strategies for happiness may make you a more successful salesperson.

WHAT'S THE POINT?

Pursuing a happy life is also the path to a more financially rewarding one.

CHAPTER 16

The Sad State of Happiness

A happy or unhappy life is your own creation.
Nobody else is responsible.
—Swami Satchidananda

An essential component of your ability to be successful depends on your level of happiness. That's a reason (among others) why it is important to gauge your level of happiness and to take steps to increase it if it falls short.

How Unhappy Are We?

A 2010 Gallup survey measured the happiness of citizens of various countries. The results show that citizens of prosperous countries are not necessarily happier than those in less prosperous ones. Panama ranked higher in happiness than the United States, although the gross domestic product of the United States is six times higher than Panama's. Israel, beset by the constant threat of armed conflict, and Venezuela, governed at the time by the erratic Hugo Chavez, both ranked higher than the United States.

When you dig deeper, there seems to be a pervasive level of overall unhappiness in the United States, despite our relative wealth. One survey found that most people in the United States reported being unhappy at work. A 2006 study by Pew Research found that only about one-third of Americans are "very happy." A minority of those who attended church weekly reported being very happy. Married people are happier than unmarried people, but the majority of those in both groups report being unhappy.

Since 1972 the average level of happiness for women has dropped, while the average level of happiness for men has increased. Men become more happy as they age, but women become less happy.

The Mysterious Failure to Pursue Happiness

I have never met anyone who does not want to be happy. Yet few of us take concrete steps to move toward that goal.

While writing this book, I engaged in a very unscientific survey. I asked as many people as I could to tell me if they were happy. The majority said they weren't. Then I asked this question: "What makes you unhappy?" Not a single person failed to give me a specific response to this query. Many were unhappy at work. Some were in bad relationships. Others wanted to spend more time looking after their health through diet or exercise. Another common reason was an inability to spend more time with friends and family.

I was surprised by some of the results of my little survey. The fact that a lot of people were unhappy was consistent with other data I found. The goal of happiness is central to our core being. It's even enshrined in the Declaration of Independence: "We hold these truths to be self-evident, that all men are created equal, that they are endowed by their Creator with certain unalienable Rights, that among these are Life, Liberty and the pursuit of Happiness." Surely, making changes to achieve this goal should not be too great a burden. But without exception, none of the people I talked to about their happiness had made any adjustments to improve their situation.

In fact, highly intelligent people often double-down on activities that make them unhappy, to the exclusion of alternatives that could make them much happier. The hard-charging executive may sacrifice family life (and all other activities) to climb up the corporate ladder. When his hard work pays off with promotions and more income (well beyond what he needs to meet his family's daily needs), he works even harder, neglecting his health and his family even more. He takes more elaborate vacations and buys a bigger house, a fancier car, and a second (or third) home, yet he still feels unfulfilled and unhappy. This cycle of unhappiness can be very frustrating.

Don't Plan for Unhappiness

Why don't we make the changes that would increase our happiness? Because it takes much less effort to be unhappy. The lack of a plan for happiness becomes, by default, a prescription for unhappiness.

Celestine Chua, a personal excellence coach, offers the following suggestions for those committed to unhappiness:

- Complain a lot and focus on bad things happening in your life.

- Avoid dealing with your problems by denying their existence or procrastinating.

- Compare yourself unfavorably to others.

- Anticipate problems that may never come into existence (preferably obsess over them).

- Succumb to your problems and let them overtake your life.

- Continue to engage in activities or relationships that make you unhappy.

- Continue your efforts to change others. (You can practically insure a life of frustration and unhappiness with this tip alone.)

- Try to please everyone all the time.

- Attach yourself inflexibly to people, goals, and outcomes.

Other suggestions for an unhappy life include constantly striving and ignoring the joy of the journey. You could probably come up with your own list.

Famed self-help guru Deepak Chopra suggests reasons why so many people seem to be committed to a goal of unhappiness:

- Low self-image

- The appeal of martyrdom
- Inner conflict and confusion
- A belief that suffering is good for you
- Depression and anxiety
- Feeling trapped by circumstances
- Living with high stress
- Resistance to being healthy

Chopra believes that many of us are in a pattern of subtle self-destruction, with the inevitable goal of remaining unhappy in our lives.

One thing is very clear: there are a lot of unhappy people. If you are one of them, or if you want to improve your level of happiness, read on. There's a road map to happiness—and to improving your sales—in the following chapters.

WHAT'S THE POINT?

Without a plan for increasing your happiness, you may be consigning yourself to a life of unhappiness.

CHAPTER 17

Eliminate the Source of Unhappiness

Expecting the world to treat you fairly because you are a good
person is a little like expecting a bull not to
attack you because you are a vegetarian.

—Dennis Wholey

In the previous chapter I pointed out that many people drift along in a state of unhappiness. They lack the will to change and a plan for doing so. You don't have to be one of them. Improving your level of happiness begins with identifying what's making you unhappy and working to change it.

Identify Your Unhappiness Triggers

If you don't know what is making you unhappy, you need to find out. You could begin this process by speaking with family members, trusted friends, or members of the clergy. Sometimes writing your thoughts in a journal and rereading them can provide enlightenment. You may see the same patterns repeated over time, like an inability to get along with coworkers or a tendency to befriend people who make you feel inadequate and insecure.

If these efforts don't bear fruit, therapy can help you find the reasons for your unhappiness. You may be surprised to learn that what you think is making you unhappy is just a symptom, not the cause. Any therapy by a competent professional is probably better than none, and no one type of therapy is right for everyone. However, considerable research supports the benefits of cognitive therapy.

Cognitive therapy has the advantage of being "simple, quick, practical and goal oriented," according to an article in *Time* magazine. A major benefit of cognitive therapy is its focus on solutions, which makes the number of sessions shorter and less expensive than traditional therapy. According to the Academy of Cognitive Therapy (ACT), your therapist should be able to give you an estimate after one or two sessions. Some patients may see results in only six to eight sessions.

Although it's relatively inexpensive compared to other therapy, the cost of cognitive therapy may still seem high. But think of it this way: most people don't hesitate to spend money on things that will have little effect on resolving their unhappiness. Is the possibility of achieving happiness worth more to you than a large-screen TV?

You may qualify for free or low-cost treatment by participating in a clinical trial sponsored by the National Institute of Mental Health (NIMH). The NIMH website provides links to studies that are currently recruiting participants. The ACT website includes links to providers who offer low-cost treatment to those who meet designated criteria.

If you don't really understand the cause of your unhappiness, take the first step toward finding out. It takes courage, but the potential payoff could be a game changer.

Take Steps Toward Change

There are many possible causes of unhappiness, including poor health, bad relationships, and having a lack of any meaningful goals in life. Whatever problem you've identified, your next task is to take concrete steps to eliminate it—or at least improve it.

Some things may be easier to change than others. Suppose you have a friend who is judgmental and makes you feel bad about yourself. You could limit the time spent with this person by turning down invitations to meet. Use the time to engage in new activities where you might meet people who would make a positive contribution to your life.

Is your job making you unhappy? You are not alone. A comprehensive survey of 27,587 people explored the happiness level of employees in various jobs. Those employed in low-skill, manual, and service occupations (especially in the food and beverage industries) reported low job satisfaction.

If you're unhappy in your job and quitting is not a practical option, don't give up hope. Look for ways to make the best of your situation. The strategy you choose will depend on the basis for your unhappiness at work. Here are some possibilities to consider:

Change your job responsibilities. Talk to your manager or supervisor and see if there are opportunities for promotion or a transfer. If your problem relates to a coworker or to your boss, see if there is a possibility of working with someone else or transferring to a different department.

Consider retraining. Explore the possibility of retraining so that you might qualify for another position. Some companies will pay the cost of continuing education and retraining.

Get feedback. Ask for feedback on how you are doing in your job. Both positive and negative feedback can be valuable. Inquire whether you might be in line for a raise or what you would have to do in order to qualify for more pay.

Alleviate overwork. If you feel you are overworked, organize a presentation demonstrating your views and offering solutions for resolving the issue. Present it to your supervisor. Be prepared to explain how your proposed solutions will benefit your employer.

Unfortunately, there are situations in which none of these options will solve your problem. If so, confront that reality and start looking for another job.

Confronting My Unhappiness

I confronted the issue of trying to attain a higher level of happiness in my own life. In telling this story, I am acutely aware that many Americans are coping with real economic challenges these days. Their struggles make an abstract discussion of pursuing happiness seem shallow and trivial. For them, putting food on the table and staying in their homes is their preoccupation. The stress of their lives far exceeds anything I have experienced.

For many years, I was modestly successful but unhappy and restless. Like many lawyers, I worked long, hard hours that took me away from my family. Trying to strike the right balance between my career and my family was difficult. Spending time with family can be deferred, while the demands of practicing law seem unrelenting and inflexible. No matter how hard I worked and how well I did, I still felt unsatisfied. I was achieving my financial goals and providing nicely for my family. Yet there was a feeling of emptiness and lack of fulfillment. I was consumed with these thoughts:

- Is this all there is? I work; I come home exhausted. I get up and then start all over again.

- What is the purpose of my activity and my life? I increase the wealth of entities that are already wealthy.

- When I die, will anyone other than my immediate family and few friends and colleagues know I was here? I am not leaving any meaningful footprints in the sand.

- Is life supposed to feel like an endless grind? Where's the payoff?

These concerns troubled me for many years. I tentatively explored my issues with close friends and family. I know it sounds trite, but really what I was asking was, "Isn't my life supposed to have meaning greater than what I am experiencing?" The answer I received to my lament of "What's it all about?" was "This *is* it. It's not about anything."

My restlessness remained. In some ways, my feelings intensified. I now had a "disease" for which I was told there was no cure. This was not a happy prospect.

Then I started representing investors who had lost a significant portion of their savings due to flagrant misconduct by their stockbrokers. I found this work very satisfying, but also frustrating. In some cases, I was able to recover their money. In many others, I failed. Investors who use brokers in this country are required to submit all disputes to mandatory arbitration administered by the Financial Industry Regulatory Authority (known as FINRA). Many believe these arbitrations are biased and rigged against investors. I had a number of cases for worthy clients whose savings had been decimated by indefensible broker conduct. More often than not, they were awarded nothing by the FINRA arbitration panels. But when I was successful, I felt I had made a positive impact on my clients' lives.

That gave me both satisfaction and an idea. What if I could keep people from being victimized? I would need to demystify investing and provide simple choices that anyone could implement. Over many months of research and reflection, I came up with the concept for what turned into the first of a series of "*Smartest*" books. Instead of dealing with one investor at a time, I was able to create books that were read by tens of thousands of investors all over the world. One book was even translated into Chinese.

I started getting e-mails from readers telling me how my books had changed their lives. Some told heart-wrenching stories of how they were victimized by their stockbrokers. Others said they gave copies of my books to their children and wished it had been available when they were younger. I remember one e-mail from someone who said he bought fifty copies of one of my books and gave them out to family, friends, neighbors, and anyone else he cared about.

I didn't realize it at the time, but that restless fire was beginning to abate. I focused on writing more books that readers might find helpful in their lives. This book stems from the same motivation. For me, engaging in this activity is the gift that keeps on giving. While I still believe I could do more, and I certainly could be a better, kinder, and less judgmental person (old habits die hard), I no longer ask the questions that so troubled me before. I can't put a price on the positive feedback I receive almost daily. It has made me a happy person, content with my life, and deeply appreciative.

I was not surprised to find that authors have one of the highest ratings for job happiness.

In alleviating my unhappiness, I followed the process I have described in this chapter. I identified the problem (no direction, little meaning in life) and worked through the issues until I was able to change it. You can do the same thing.

WHAT'S THE POINT?

Find out the source of your unhappiness and work to change it.

CHAPTER 18

Make Positive Changes to Increase Happiness

If you want others to be happy, practice compassion. If you want to be happy, practice compassion.

—Dalai Lama

D o you really have the power to increase your happiness? Experts say yes. Sonja Lyubomirsky, a social psychologist and author of *The How of Happiness: A Scientific Approach to Getting the Life You Want*, believes that like all of us, you were born with a "genetic set point" that determines 50 percent of your happiness level. In other words, to some extent you tend to be happier or unhappier than other people simply by your nature. An additional 10 percent of your happiness level is imposed by circumstances like health, economic status, and marital status. The encouraging finding is that you are in total control of the balance of 40 percent. It should be very comforting to learn that you have the ability to make such a large contribution to your own happiness.

The previous chapter talked about changing the situations that are making you unhappy. Those situations are uniquely your own. But no matter who you are and what circumstances you find yourself in, you can also boost your happiness by adopting some simple habits and practices in your daily life.

Prioritize Happiness

According to Shawn Achor, author of *The Happiness Advantage*, happiness is a choice well within your power to make. He believes the brain can initially scan for positive or negative meanings in the input it receives. The problem arises when your brain is programmed (by you) to scan first for the negative. Achor believes the brain can be trained to first scan for the positive. He suggests some simple practices to help you retrain your brain. One is to exercise for at least ten minutes every day. Another is meditating, which I discuss in Chapter 19. He also recommends making it a daily practice to write down things that make you happy, things for which you are grateful, or one positive experience you had over the last twenty-four hours.

Make Emotional Connections

In Chapter 8, I discussed the importance of making an emotional connection in sales. Emotional connections are also an essential component of your level of happiness. There is ample evidence that we are happier when we are with other people than when we are alone. Happiness makes us more pleasant, helpful, and sociable.

We have social interactions every day. We serve the needs of others and they serve us. As you go through your day, try to make as many emotional connections as you can.

It's easy to make those connections. For example, I was recently at an electronics store. The person helping me was greeting some customers in English and others in Spanish. I asked about her background and why she was working there. That simple inquiry transformed an otherwise routine experience into an enriching one for both of us. She told me about growing up in Santo Domingo, her goals, and her aspirations. I found her to be extremely impressive. She was touched that I asked about her. If you make a similar effort to connect with others, you will be surprised at how enriching these encounters can be for both of you.

Practice Empathy

You are already aware of how potent empathy is in the sales context (see Chapter 5). Empathy can also increase your level of happiness. When you demonstrate empathy, life becomes more meaningful. There is evidence that empathetic people have more successful marriages and more substantive social relationships. CEOs who demonstrate empathy are more successful. Teachers who are empathetic have students who test better. Empathetic doctors have healthier patients. Empathetic people tend to live longer. No wonder having empathy makes people happier.

You have ample opportunities in your business and personal life to express empathy. A customer service representative could be empathetic by acknowledging the problem, showing understanding and concern, and offering a solution instead of arguing with the customer over who is right. In your personal life, when confronted with a friend who is upset, you could indicate that you understand why he is so upset and that you would have the same feelings if you were in his situation.

Become a Genuine Listener

I discussed the power of listening when you are selling in Chapter 11. Listening has the added benefit of increasing your happiness. This makes perfect sense. It's difficult to develop empathy if you are not listening. Without empathy, you can't make an emotional connection. Without an emotional connection, you can't develop meaningful relationships. And without meaningful relationships, you are unlikely to achieve a higher level of happiness.

There are many other benefits of practicing genuine, or reflective, listening, but the primary one is conveying to others that you sincerely care about them. Remember to let others speak for as long as they wish without interruption, to listen intently, and to respond in a way that demonstrates both your understanding of what is being said and the emotions the speaker is expressing. Dalmar Fisher, in *Communication in Organizations*, gives an example of how to listen reflectively when a friend expresses concern over the possibility of losing a job. Fisher recommends saying,

"It's scary" rather than "Maybe the cutbacks won't affect you."

Feel the Power of Giving

Studies show that we derive far more pleasure from giving than receiving. Women with multiple sclerosis who volunteered to listen compassionately to other patients developed increased self-esteem, greater self-acceptance, and higher satisfaction over the three years of the study. They benefited even more than those they were helping.

The evidence linking generosity to a happier life is overwhelming. An article in the *Christian Science Monitor* referenced five hundred studies demonstrating the power of unselfish love. One study looked at one hundred communities in England, ranging from inner cities to rural villages. Communities with the highest levels of volunteerism had less crime, better schools, and happier, healthier residents. These effects apply with equal force to countries all over the world.

Studies of young children have shown they are happier sharing their treats with a puppet than consuming them. Another study suggests that just thinking about giving to a charity can bring you pleasure. It causes increased activity in the part of the brain that stimulates "feel-good" chemicals like serotonin and dopamine.

We can learn a lot about acts of kindness from our children. When Taylor Marie Crabtree was only seven, she started a business selling hand-painted hair clips at local stores. She used the money to buy teddy bears for children with cancer. Once the story got out, donations poured in. She raised her goal from five hundred teddy bears to seven hundred. Taylor's extraordinary generosity has touched many recipients, and it has given Taylor a completely different perspective on life. She has enriched herself and many others. All this sprang from an idea and a desire to help those less fortunate.

Taylor may be onto something she may not have contemplated. When children engage in acts of kindness, evidence shows they become happier and well liked. There is no reason the same result would not be achieved by adults. The opportunities for giving are many: donating to charities, devoting time to a hospice, volunteering at a hospital or nursing home, spending time at a shelter for battered women or the homeless, delivering meals to those who are housebound, building homes with organizations like Habitat for Humanity, taking a meal to a sick neighbor, calling a relative just to find out how they're doing, and many, many others.

Focus on Experiences

There is ample evidence that pleasurable experiences, rather than material possessions, are a source of happiness. The possibilities for positive experiences are almost endless. One blog lists hundreds of examples. They include enjoying special meals, observing beauty in nature and art, listening to great music, taking trips, and sharing activities with friends.

Why do experiences make us happier than possessions? The authors of one study suggest it's because experiences have a more powerful effect on us. Who can't recall a first love, or a special vacation, or attending a moving talk or concert? Material possessions don't have that kind of long-lasting impact on our memories.

Pursue Your Passions

All of us share this in common: we each have a passion for something. Whatever your passion is, it gives you more pleasure than buying a new car or being praised by others.

You feel better when you pursue this activity. In fact, if you asked yourself to list your happiest times, the pursuit of your passion would probably make the list.

I have a friend who loves nothing more than to camp out and hike in our beautiful national parks. Another colleague is an engineer, but his passion is music. He spends much of his leisure time recording music that is unlikely to be heard by anyone other than himself and his friends. I am a lifelong tennis player. Once a week I take lessons from a wonderful teacher. I will never be recognized as a great tennis player, but I eagerly look forward to each lesson.

It doesn't matter if your passion is gardening, fishing, hunting, or painting. What is important is that you allocate time to pursue your passion. Doing so will contribute to your happiness.

Add Play

One study measured "playfulness" in adults, defined as "the predisposition to engage in playful activities and interactions." It found that playfulness relates positively to an overall feeling of well-being and quality of life, among other benefits.

How can you be more playful? Loosen up. Joke around. Make fun of yourself. Engage in spontaneous behavior. Be unpredictable. Clown around. Don't take yourself or others so seriously. It's good for you.

I am not suggesting that you quit work and spend all your time playing. But you can cut yourself some slack, relax, appreciate what really matters, and have some fun. The collateral benefits are significant.

Look After Your Health

Poor health correlates highly with unhappiness. While some health issues may be beyond your control, many are not. There is ample evidence that heart disease, diabetes, colon cancer, hip fractures, and high blood pressure, among other chronic illnesses, can be prevented or improved through diet and exercise. Up to 60 percent of cancer cases are related to poor diet. If you want to be happy, take responsibility for remaining in good health.

It's Up to You

You can choose to be happy, with all of the benefits of happiness: less stress, a feeling of contentment and fulfillment, a sense of well-being. And here's the kicker: the happier you are, the more likely you are to achieve success. You can enjoy your work more, will probably work less, and can appreciate every day of your life for the wonderful gift that it is.

WHAT'S THE POINT?

You have the power to increase your level of happiness.

CHAPTER 19

Meditate

Meditation. . . dissolves the mind. It erases itself.
Throws the ego out on its big brittle ass.
—Tom Robbins

I have an uncle who is ninety-two years old. He is in excellent physical condition and mentally very acute. He plays squash and tennis four times a week. He works every day in his business, producing and distributing educational films. He travels extensively for business and pleasure. His real name is Myron, but he never liked that name. Everyone calls him "Mike." Mike has been meditating for as long as I can remember.

He has a mantra: "Don't hurry, don't worry, we are only here for a short time." Until recently, my mantra was the opposite: "Hurry, worry, we don't have enough time." Wherever I was, I was thinking about where I wanted to be.

I run every day. I live in a beautiful gated community in Southwest Florida, where I am surrounded by the wonders of nature, including eagles, egrets, blue herons, and a variety of other birds. My run is a feast for the eyes, but I never used to see any of it. When I started my run, I was focused on when it would be over. My brain was consumed with all the things I had to do when I returned to my office. I would even take my cell phone with me so I would not miss any calls. I could not enjoy the present because I was so intensely focused on the future.

The concept of "doing nothing" was alien to me. I always had more things to do than time to accomplish the tasks that awaited me. I can't remember any time when I was still and just reveled in living moment to moment, appreciating what was happening right now without wishing that I was working on my "to do" list.

I did not start meditating until I did the research for this book. I read a book by Jon Kabat-Zinn called *Full Catastrophe Living*. This book was an eye-opener for me. I then ordered four CDs, narrated by the author, that serve as a guide to meditation and to some very simple, nonstressful yoga exercises.

How I Meditate

I try to meditate every day. I started with five minutes and worked my way up to twenty minutes. Sometimes, when I use the CDs, I expand my meditation time to forty-five minutes. I go into a room and close the door. I make sure I can't be disturbed by anything, including the telephone or the beeping that indicates new e-mails have arrived. I put my iPhone in "airplane" mode and set the timer. I set the alert sound to "harp," which is a gentle and pleasing reminder that my allotted time for meditation has ended.

I dim the lights in the room. I sit in an erect posture and gently close my eyes. I focus on my breathing, paying particular attention to the rise of my stomach on the in-breath and how it goes down on the out-breath. Every time a distracting thought pops into my head, I just observe the fact that this thought exists and go back to being aware of my breathing. I don't change my breathing. I just remain intently focused on it. No matter how many times other thoughts intrude, I repeat the process of observing them, letting them go, and going back to being aware of the repetitive process of breathing in and breathing out.

I don't try to achieve anything, an attitude that is critical to meditation. Having goals—like trying to relax or lowering your blood pressure—creates stress, which is the antithesis of meditation. I just follow the simple plan of sitting quietly and focusing on my breathing.

How Meditation Benefits Me

From my very first meditation session, I had an immense feeling of relief and relaxation. I could feel the muscles in my face relax. I reveled in the luxury of "doing nothing." I experienced an involuntary smile within the first minute of meditating. I understood for the first time that it was okay to take a few minutes of every day and focus on myself, without that nagging feeling that I should be doing something else.

The carryover effects were immediate and profound. I became more conscious of the present and less focused on the future. Now when I run, I see what is around me and appreciate the raw beauty of nature. I am no longer preoccupied with finishing my run. I just enjoy the experience. Sometimes I stop to take a look at something particularly stunning, like a wood stork or an eagle. In the past, I would have barely noticed them. The best way I can describe my feelings is that all the colors of nature seem brighter.

Beginner's Mind

There is a concept in meditation called "beginner's mind." It describes having the same view of the world that a child does. The goal is to look at everything as if you are viewing it for the first time.

In his book, Jon Kabat-Zinn gives an example of handing participants three raisins. Instead of consuming them all at once, they view each raisin like they have never seen or tasted one before. They examine it carefully, noting its unique characteristics. They chew each one slowly, appreciating its texture and flavor.

The concept of "beginner's mind" is the best way to describe the effect of meditation. It slows everything down and permits you to enjoy and appreciate "what is" instead of "what should be."

Evidence-Based Benefits of Meditation

Of all the subjects I researched for this book, the data on the beneficial effects of meditation were the most compelling. Over five million people worldwide practice meditation. It's discussed in over six hundred research studies. The results of these studies have been published in more than a hundred journals. Here are some of the research findings about the benefits of meditation:

Empathy. There is ample evidence that meditation acts to stimulate the area of the brain responsible for empathy and compassion. As you know, genuine listening and empathy play critical roles both in making you a successful salesperson and in increasing your level of happiness. One study used functional magnetic resonance imaging to measure the brain circuits used to detect emotions and feelings. It found that meditation changed these brain circuits, making the participants more empathetic and compassionate. Another study found that the portion of the brain associated with empathy was more strongly activated in people who meditated than in those who didn't.

Health. According to the Mayo Clinic, meditation reduces stress by giving you a new perspective, increasing your self-awareness, and reducing negative emotions, among other benefits. The clinic also notes research indicating that meditation may help a number of medical conditions, including depression, fatigue, high blood pressure, and insomnia.

One study aggregated the data from nine other published studies. It found that blood pressure dropped significantly in those practicing meditation compared to those who did not.

Another study found that among African American patients at high risk for cardiovascular disease, those who regularly meditated reduced their risk of heart attacks, strokes and mortality from all causes by 43 percent, compared to a comparable group that received education about diet and lifestyle without meditation training.

Intelligence. Meditation may make you smarter. One study found that the hippocampus area of the brain, which is associated with learning and memory, increased in density after participants had engaged in thirty minutes of meditation each day for eight weeks. Similar changes did not occur in a control group that did not meditate. A study done at UCLA found that participants who engaged in long-term meditation experienced changes in their brains related to the ability to process information more quickly.

Creativity. Another study looked at how meditation techniques affect "divergent thinking" and "convergent thinking." Divergent thinking permits you to come up with new ideas. Convergent thinking permits you to choose the single best answer to a given problem, like identifying a common link in a number of different words. Both types of thinking can be positively impacted by meditation.

Reduction in pain. It's difficult to succeed in sales, or to achieve any level of happiness, if you have chronic pain. This is another area where meditation may be helpful. One study tested participants who were given only one hour of meditation training. In a controlled experiment, meditation increased activity in areas of the brain that reduce the perception of pain. Researchers found that meditation produced a greater reduction in pain than morphine.

Happiness. Given these benefits, it is not surprising that those who have followed a meditation regimen seem to be calmer and happier than those who don't. There is a scientific basis for this difference. Brain scans demonstrate that meditators' brain activity shows a significant shift in activity to the left frontal lobe and less activity in the amygdala, where the brain processes fear.

All these are just some of the benefits of meditation. In my case, I found that meditating made me calmer and more patient. Once I understood it was okay to be mindful of the moment (instead of reliving the past or projecting the future), I became more focused and analytical. I saw things with greater clarity. I gained perspective. I felt more empowered and in control of my life. I learned that "doing nothing" can be much more powerful than always "doing something."

WHAT'S THE POINT?

The daily practice of meditation is likely to make you a better salesperson and increase your level of happiness.

CHAPTER 20

Make It Happen

Despite good intentions, most goals go unfulfilled.
—Amy N. Dalton and Stephen A. Spiller

The traits and strategies for becoming happier and a more successful salesperson are not difficult to understand. However, changing entrenched patterns of behavior can be challenging. For example, if you are accustomed to making presentations and having others rely on your advice, becoming a genuine listener may be difficult for you. If you view closing a sale as using manipulative phrases, it will take some practice to put yourself in the shoes of your prospective customer and *really* understand her point of view. If you are an "alpha male," understanding how to communicate effectively with women may be especially difficult. Here are some tips to help you implement the strategies discussed in this book.

Plan to Achieve Your Goals of Happiness and Success

The first step in achieving your goals is to identify the traits you need to adopt and the strategies you need to implement. Then devise a plan. You may be familiar with the saying that "those who fail to plan, plan to fail."

Research confirms that having good intentions is not enough. One study involved college students whose goal was to increase their fruit intake by eating one piece of fruit every day for a couple of weeks. Those who planned in advance where and how they would eat their fruit were more likely to achieve their goal, even though everyone was equally committed. Similar results were found for other goals, like exercising, smoking cessation, recycling, and doing well in school.

Your plan should be both detailed in scope and realistic in practice. According to a study by the office of human resources at Dartmouth College, you are more likely to achieve your goals if they are:

- Measurable
- Achievable
- Specific
- Time-based
- Energizing
- Relevant

Adopt an Optimistic Attitude

A number of studies demonstrate that those who are optimistic about achieving their goals are more persistent, exert more effort, and are more willing to adjust their goals instead of abandoning them altogether. This research is consistent with many other studies finding the benefit of what is called "dispositional optimism." That means the tendency to expect positive future outcomes (based on realistic facts and probabilities, not fantasies, as discussed in Chapter 1). People with this outlook tend to be less stressed, better able to cope with stress, and more successful academically and professionally. They are also likely to be more successful in their personal relationships.

Are you a pessimist? Do a quick self-check:

- Do you believe bad things are inevitable in your life?

- Do you believe all (or almost all) events in your life will have a bad ending?

- Do you believe that when bad things do happen, it's your fault?

If you said "yes" to each of these questions, you are definitely a pessimist. The essence of being a pessimist is the belief that failure is the likely outcome.

Converting from pessimism to optimism is a worthy goal, but it's not easy. Pessimistic reactions are subconscious choices. To change them requires understanding the basis for your feelings that negative consequences are inevitable. Unless you are successful in reversing your pessimistic outlook, it's unlikely you will be able to reach your goals. Cognitive therapy (which I discussed in Chapter 17) can be effective in reducing negative thinking and possibly increasing positive views.

If you are a pessimist, seek help in banishing the negativity that is keeping you from reaching your full potential. Learn how to adopt a more optimistic view of life. The benefits could be significant.

Address Other Psychological Issues

Aside from pessimism, other psychological issues may be impeding you from achieving your goals. Some issues may have underlying causes. If you don't resolve those issues, you may not be able to implement your plan.

For example, as I have discussed, the ability to be empathetic is critical to your ability to succeed in sales. Up to 16 percent of patients in clinical settings are diagnosed with narcissistic personality disorder, which is characterized by lack of empathy. According to the American Psychiatric Association, someone with this disorder "is unwilling to recognize or identify with the feelings and needs of others." If your inability to give credence to others' feelings is caused by an underlying psychological disorder, you may need professional help to resolve it.

Don't Try to Fix Everything at Once

Marshall Goldsmith, a prolific author and management coach, recommends that you work on changing only one behavior pattern at a time, starting with the one that you believe will make the most profound impact. Based on his experience, trying to change more than one behavior at a time is too overwhelming.

To help you choose which behavior to work on, try to identify the benefit of making the change. Goldsmith recommends completing the sentence "When I get better at . . ." You might say, for instance, "When I get better at being open to differing opinions, I will hear more great ideas." This exercise helps you identify the change that will bring the most benefit. Other behaviors you might want to change could include being too judgmental, interrupting, not listening, not asking questions, or not being empathetic.

Don't Get Overwhelmed

Here's a tip I use myself: break down big projects into a series of mini-tasks. Here's an example of how I do it. When I am confronted with writing a new book, I always feel overwhelmed. I have written six books. I know the process all too well. Depending on the amount of research involved, it can take up to a year to finish the first draft. Then comes still more work: rewriting, editing, fact-checking, formatting, checking the footnotes, doing supplemental research, submitting the manuscript to my publisher, doing more edits and revisions, responding to copyedits, and drafting the cover copy. It is a grueling, daunting process. The biggest barrier to getting started is knowing what a long, arduous journey it is to the finish line.

Instead of being paralyzed by the enormity of what confronts me, I view it as a series of small steps. I try to make each step attainable. I allot a few days to do the research for one chapter. I try to write five hundred words a day. Setting that goal changes the project from "completing a book" to "writing five hundred words." Completing a book is overwhelming. Writing five hundred words is fairly easy. That's about the length of an average blog post. I am confident I can do that.

The process becomes self-fulfilling. Once I have a good start on a first draft, I feel momentum building. As I do research, it usually leads me in new directions. Writing comes much more easily once I have made some progress and have a direction.

It's time to make your plan. Go back and review my suggestions for increasing your happiness and becoming a more successful salesperson. Identify the traits and strategies you want to adopt. Develop specific goals and action steps, listing them in order of priority based on what you believe will have the most meaningful impact. Don't start on the second task until you have finished the first one. Continue down the list until you have covered them all.

We have taken this journey together. I am confident that you have a sound road map for a happier, more fulfilling life.

WHAT'S THE POINT?

To become happier and more successful requires *both* an understanding of what needs to change and a plan for implementing those changes.

Need More Convincing?

It is important for you to be aware of the research underlying the views and recommendations in this book. I am aware of the temptation to "cherry-pick" studies that support my views and ignore contrary data. As I did my research, I adopted the views of the studies I found most compelling. I did not make an effort to reference every study that is contrary to these views. If you are interested in getting a broader perspective, the studies I cited will give you an excellent starting point.

Here are the sources I used for each chapter in this book.

Chapter 1: Pragmatism

Data concerning the size of the self-help industry can be found in the abstract of this report: Marketdata Enterprises

Inc., *The US Market for Self-Improvement Products and Services*, September 1, 2006, available at www.marketresearch.com/Marketdata-Enterprises-Inc-v416/Self-Improvement-Products-Services-1338280.

Steven Novella's dim views of the self-help industry are set forth in his post "Firewalk Mishap" on *NeuroLogica Blog*, July 23, 2012, http://theness.com/neurologicablog/index.php/firewalk-mishap.

In his book *59 Seconds: Think a Little, Change a Lot* (New York: Knopf, 2009), psychologist Richard Wiseman debunks many of the myths of the self-help industry.

Emily Roberts's views on self-esteem and self-confidence are set forth in her blog post "The Difference Between Self-Esteem and Self-Confidence," *HealthyPlace*, May 2, 2012, www.healthyplace.com/blogs/buildingselfesteem/2012/05/the-difference-between-self-esteem-and-self-confidence.

Quotes from Brain Tracy and his views on the importance of self-esteem can be found in "Self-Esteem and Sales Success," *Brian Tracy's Blog*, November 7, 2007, www.briantracy.com/blog/sales-success/self-esteem-and-sales-success.

THE SMARTEST SALES BOOK YOU'LL EVER READ 209

The quote from French psychologist Émile Coué was referenced by Joanne V. Wood, PhD, in "Should We Rethink Positive Thinking? Giving Ourselves Pep Talks May Backfire," *Psychology Today*, March 20, 2009, www.psychologytoday.com/blog/regarding-self-regard/200903/should-we-re-think-positive-thinking.

You can find the biography of Tomas Chamorro-Premuzic, PhD, at www.psychologytoday.com/experts/tomas-chamorro-premuzic-phd. His blog post on the *Harvard Business Review* website is "Less-Confident People Are More Successful," July 6, 2012, http://blogs.hbr.org/cs/2012/07/less_confident_people_are_more_su.html.

The study showing that preoccupation with self-esteem has many negative consequences is *Self-Confidence: Intrapersonal Strategies* by Roland Benabou and Jean Tirole, December 1999, available at www.econ.yale.edu/seminars/microt/mt00/benabou100040 4.pdf.

The study that failed to show a link between boosting self-esteem and better job performance is reported in "Does High Self-Esteem Cause Better Performance, Interpersonal Success, Happiness, or Healthier Lifestyles?" by Roy F.

Baumeister, Jennifer D. Campbell, Joachim I. Krueger, and Kathleen D. Vohs, *Psychological Science in the Public Interest* 4, no. 1 (May 2003): 1-44, http://psi.sagepub.com/content/4/1/1.short.

The views of Heidi Grant Halvorson on self-esteem are set forth in her blog post on the *Harvard Business Review* website, "To Succeed, Forget Self-Esteem," September 20, 2012, http://blogs.hbr.org/cs/2012/09/to_succeed_forget_self-esteem.html.

For a study showing the benefits of self-compassion, see Kristin D. Neff, Stephanie S. Rude, and Kristin L. Kirkpatrick, "An Examination of Self-Compassion in Relation to Positive Psychological Functioning and Personality Traits," *Journal of Research in Personality* 41, no. 4 (August 2007): 908–16, available at www.sciencedirect.com/science/article/pii/S009265660600095X.

A study showing that self-compassion motivates people to achieve their goals is Juliana G. Breines and Serena Chen, "Self-Compassion Increases Self-Improvement Motivation," *Personality and Social Psychology Bulletin* 38, no. 9 (September 2012): 1133–43, available at http://psp.sagepub.com/content/38/9/1133.abstract.

A summary of a research paper by Nicholas Emler on the causes of low self-esteem can be found in "The Costs and Causes of Low Self-Esteem," *Findings* (publication of the Joseph Rowntree Foundation), November 2001, www.jrf.org.uk/sites/files/jrf/n71.pdf.

A study that questions the enthusiasm for changing self-esteem and reviews available research on this subject is Nicholas Emler, *Self-Esteem: The Costs and Causes of Low Self-Worth* (York, UK: Joseph Rowntree Foundation, 2001), www.jrf.org.uk/sites/files/jrf/1859352510.pdf.

For an excellent article that debunks many of the myths of self-help gurus, see Annie Murphy Paul, "Self-Help: Shattering the Myths," *Psychology Today*, March 1, 2001, www.psychologytoday.com/articles/200103/self-help-shattering-the-myths.

The study showing the difference between visualizing a goal and visualizing what it will take to achieve that goal is Lien B. Pham and Shelley E. Taylor, "From Thought to Action: Effects of Process- Versus Outcome-Based Mental Simulations on Performance," *Personality and Social Psychology Bulletin* 25, no. 2 (February 1999): 250–60, available at http://psp.sagepub.com/content/25/2/250.abstract.

The plight of those burned walking over hot coals at the Anthony Robbins event was reported by Oliver Burkeman in "The Power of Negative Thinking," *New York Times*, August 4, 2012, www.nytimes.com/2012/08/05/opinion/sunday/the-positive-power-of-negative-thinking.html.

For a discussion of the science behind walking over a burning bed of coals, see Jennifer Ouellette's blog post on the *Scientific American* website, "Come Firewalk with Me: The Physics of Hot Coals," July 24, 2012, http://blogs.scientificamerican.com/cocktail-party-physics/2012/07/24/come-firewalk-with-me-the-physics-of-hot-coals.

No one should ever attempt to walk on burning coals. It can cause serious injury. If you must, be sure your feet are very wet. As you walk on the coals, the moisture on your feet will evaporate and form a protective gas layer. This process is described by Ted Pavlic in the "Ask the Experts" feature on the PhysLink.com website, www.physlink.com/education/askexperts/ae580.cfm.

The distinction between positivity in expectations versus fantasies is set forth by Gabriele Oettingen and Doris Mayer in "Motivating Function of Thinking about the Future: Expectations Versus Fantasies," *Journal of*

Personality and Social Psychology 83, no. 5 (November 2002): 1198–1212, available at http://bit.ly/Xt2wyB.

For a discussion of problems with fantasizing about goals, see Kate Reilly's post on the *Psych Your Mind* blog, "Perils of Positive Thinking," July 23, 2012, http://psych-your-mind.blogspot.ca/2012/07/perils-of-positive-thinking.html.

Chapter 2: Honesty

For opinions of the public about salespeople, see John Patania, "Perception of Salespeople," Biznik.com, September 25, 2009, http://biznik.com/articles/perception-of-salespeople.

The survey of corporate buyers is reported by Bradford Thomas, Simon Mitchell, and Jeff Del Rossa in *Sales: Strategic Partnership or Necessary Evil?* (2007–2008 Global Sales Perceptions Report), DDI, http://66.179.232.89/pdf/globalsalesperceptionsreport_br_d di.pdf.

The survey of venture capitalists indicating the importance of honesty is referenced by Richard M. White in *The Entrepreneur's Manual* (Radnor, PA: Chilton, 1977).

Surveys showing that honesty is the most admired trait in business leaders are discussed by James M. Kouzes and Barry Z. Posner in *The Leadership Challenge* (San Francisco: Jossey-Bass, 2008).

Research summarizing the collateral benefits of honesty is summarized by Adam Khan in "Deep Honesty: A Spiritual Path," an article on the YouMe Works website, http://youmeworks.com/deephonesty.html.

The survey of the attitudes of men and women in the securities industry is discussed by Allison Kade in "Are Women More Honest Than Men When It Comes to Finance?," *Huffington Post*, July 20, 2012, www.huffingtonpost.com/learnvest/women-more-honest-than-men-finance_b_1688937.html.

Roger Steare's study about morality in men and women is discussed by Hannah Furness in "Women Are More Moral than Men, Survey Says," *Telegraph* (UK), April 16, 2012, www.telegraph.co.uk/science/science-news/9206176/Women-are-more-moral-than-men-survey-says.html. You can find (and take) the moral DNA questionnaire at www.moraldna.org.

For the study about the perceptions of honesty in men and women, see Marilyn G. Boltz, Rebecca L. Dyer, and Anna R. Miller, "Are You Lying to Me? Temporal Cues for

THE SMARTEST SALES BOOK YOU'LL EVER READ 215

Deception," *Journal of Language and Social Psychology* 29, no. 4 (December 2010): 458–66, available at http://jls.sagepub.com/content/29/4/458.full.pdf.

For a discussion of verbal and nonverbal cues that may be perceived as indicating dishonesty, see "How to Read Body Language: Secrets and Lying" on the Essortment website, www.essortment.com/read-body-language-secrets-lying-63878.html. Other tips for detecting dishonesty can be found in "How to Recognize a Lie" on the TopTipSpot website, www.toptipspot.com/tips/people/howto/recognize-a-lie.php.

Chapter 3: Sincerity

The report from the Arthur W. Page Society is *The Authentic Enterprise* (New York: Arthur W. Page Society, 2007), www.landesassociates.com/pdfs/2007AuthenticEnterprise.pdf.

The story about the trial lawyers in South Dakota is reported by Kevin P. Durkin and Colin H. Dunn in "Building Your Case for the Jury," American Bar Association website,

http://apps.americanbar.org/litigation/litigationnews/trial_s
kills/110210-tips-jury-trial.html.

The prepared text of the Commencement address delivered by Steve Jobs on June 12, 2005 at Stanford University is available at:

http://news.stanford.edu/news/2005/june15/jobs-061505.html

The study on the effect of the perception of sincerity of real estate agents is Sandra Gountas and John Gountas, "Exploring Customer Orientation in the Real Estate: The Customer Perspective," available at

http://www.duplication.net.au/ANZMAC09/papers/ANZM
AC2009-317.pdf.

The study on the effect of the perceived sincerity of apologies by romantically involved couples is by Amy S. Ebesu Hubbard, Blake Hendrickson, Keri Szejda Fehrenbach and Jennifer Sur, "Effects of Timing and Sincerity of an Apology on Satisfaction and Changes in Negative feelings During Conflicts," *Western Journal of Communication,* Vol. 77, No. 3 (May-June 2013): 305-322, available at:

http://www.scribd.com/doc/146814951/Effects-of-Timing-and-Sincerity-of-an-Apology-on-Satisfaction-and-Changes-in-Negative-Feelings-During-Conflicts.

Chapter 4: Grit

The study on the relationship of grit to success, to SAT scores, and to achieving long- term goals is by Angela L. Duckworth, Christopher Peterson, Michael D. Matthews, and Dennis R. Kelly, "Grit: Perseverance and Passion for Long-Term Goals," *Journal of Personality and Social Psychology* 92, no. 6 (June 2007): 1087–1101, available at www.sas.upenn.edu/~duckwort/images/Grit%20JPSP.pdf.

The traits of "outliers" are discussed by Malcolm Gladwell in *Outliers: The Story of Success* (New York: Little, Brown, 2008).

The study relating the effect of deliberate practice to the performance skill of musicians is by K. Anders Ericsson, Ralf Th. Krampe, and Clemens Tesch-Römer, "The Role of Deliberate Practice in the Acquisition of Expert Performance," *Psychological Review* 100, no. 3 (July 1993): 363–404, available at http://graphics8.nytimes.com/images/blogs/freakonomics/pdf/DeliberatePractice%28PsychologicalReview%29.pdf.

The article by David Brooks is "Genius: The Modern View," *New York Times*, May 1, 2009, www.nytimes.com/2009/05/01/opinion/01brooks.html.

The survey on how many calls it took to close a sale is referenced by Nancy LaJoice in "Keep in Touch," available on the website of the Baltimore Washington Corridor Chamber, www.bwcc.org/WCMEDIA/DOCUMENTS/SalesMarketin g%20-%20Keep%20In%20Touch%20Article.pdf.

Chapter 5: Empathy

For an excellent article on the importance of empathy, see Julie Fuimano's "Importance of Empathy in the Workplace," *Advance for Nurses*, October 13, 2009, http://nursing.advanceweb.com/editorial/content/editorial.a spx?cc=204810.

For a discussion of the importance of empathy in psychotherapy, see Richard G. Erskine's article "Beyond Empathy: A Therapy of Contact-in-Relationship" on the Institute for Integrative Psychotherapy website, www.integrativetherapy.com/se/articles.php?id=39.   The author notes that "empathy is the foundation for inquiry, attunement and involvement."

The steps to practicing empathy can be found in an article by Lisa Brookes Kift, "5 Steps to Practicing

Empathy with your Partner," on the Talk About Marriage online forum, March 5, 2008, http://talkaboutmarriage.com/articles/872-5-steps-practicing-empathy-your-partner.html.

For a discussion of traits that make a good salesperson, see David Mayer and Herbert M. Greenberg's "What Makes a Good Salesman," *Harvard Business Review*, July–August 1964, http://hbr.org/2006/07/what-makes-a-good-salesman/ar/1. The authors of this study state, "Our basic theory is that a good salesman must have at least two basic qualities: empathy and ego drive."

For a discussion of the influence of empathy on the interaction between buyer and seller, see Rosann L. Spiro and Barton A. Weitz's "Adaptive Selling: Conceptualization, Measurement, and Nomological Validity," *Journal of Marketing Research* 27, no. 1 (February 1990): 61–69, abstract available at www.jstor.org/stable/3172551. For a study on the importance of empathy in sales generally, see David Spaulding and Richard E. Plank, "Selling Automobiles at Retail: Is Empathy Important?," *Marketing Management Journal* 17, no. 2 (Fall 2007): 142–155.

For a discussion of empathetic listening, see Susan Krauss Whitbourne's article "11 Ways That Active

Listening Can Help Your Relationships," *Psychology Today* website, March 13, 2012, www.psychologytoday.com/blog/fulfillment-any-age/201203/11-ways-active-listening-can-help-your-relationships.

You can find Stephen Covey's views on the importance of empathic listening in "Using Empathic Listening to Collaborate," an excerpt from his book *The 7 Habits of Highly Effective People* (New York: Free Press, 1989) posted on the *Fast Company* website, December 26, 2011, www.fastcompany.com/1727872/using-empathic-listening-collaborate.

Jeff Haden's views on what traits make for a charismatic person can be found in his article "10 Habits of Remarkably Charismatic People," *Inc.* magazine website, July 10, 2012, www.inc.com/jeff-haden/10-habits-of-remarkably-charismatic-people.html.

The importance of sales charisma is discussed by Liz Wendling in "Five Secrets to Sales Charisma," *ColoradoBiz* magazine website, January 26, 2011, www.cobizmag.com/articles/five-secrets-to-sale-charisma.

The study showing that brain chemistry may dispose some people to have greater empathy is by Sarina M. Rodriques, Laura R. Saslow, Natalia Garcia, Oliver P.

John, and Dacher Keltner, "Oxytocin Receptor Genetic Variation Relates to Empathy and Stress Reactivity in Humans," *Proceedings of the National Academy of Sciences* 106, no. 50 (December 15, 2009), www.pnas.org/content/106/50/21437.full.pdf.

Chapter 6: Self-Awareness

The study showing the amount of time it takes to make a first impression is Janine Willis and Alexander Todorov, "First Impressions: Making Up Your Mind After a 100-Ms Exposure to a Face," *Psychological Science* 17, no. 7 (July 2006): 592–98, available at www.consequentialstrangers.com/wp-content/uploads/2011/03/WillisTodorow2006-FirstImpressions.pdf.

The study showing the different impressions made by hairstyles is summarized by Dr. Marianne LaFrance in "Impressions" on the Peter Lamas website, www.lamasbeauty.com/beauty/september03/Impressions.htm.

The findings about the first impressions made by teeth may have been influenced by the fact that the survey was sponsored by Invisalign, a product sold to straighten teeth as an alternative to braces. Nevertheless, the methodology appears to be solid. The results are available in "Invisalign Smile Survey" at http://keltonglobal.com/images/pdf/Invisalign_Smile_Stud y-BreakOut_Report.pdf.

The study on how clothing affects first impressions is by Karen J. Pine, Ben C. Fletcher, and Neil Howlett, "The Effect of Appearance on First Impressions," executive summary available at http://karenpine.com/wp-content- /uploads/2011/09/Executive-summary_The-Effect-of- Appearance-on-First-Impressions.pdf. This study was sponsored by Mathieson & Brooke Tailors Ltd., which stood to benefit from the findings.

The study of attire during job interviews is by Cassandra Janelle Barger, "Understanding the Impact of Applicant Attire on Interviewer Perceptions" (undergraduate thesis, California State University, December 2009), available at www.csulb.edu/colleges/cba/honors/thesis/documents/Cass andra_Barger_Thesis.pdf. Other studies have reached similar conclusions, including Sandra Forsythe, Mary F. Drake, and Charles E. Cox, "Influence of Applicant's Dress on Interviewer's Selection Decisions," *Journal of Applied Psychology* 70, no. 2 (May 1985): 374–78, http://psycnet.apa.org/index.cfm?fa=buy.optionToBuy&id= 1985-23948-001 (registration required).

The study on shaking hands is by W. F. Chaplin, J. B. Phillips, J. D. Brown, N. R. Clanton, and J. L. Stein, "Handshaking, Gender, Personality, and First Impressions," *Journal of Personality and Social Psychology* 79, no. 1 (July 2000): 110–17, abstract available at www.ncbi.nlm.nih.gov/pubmed/10909881.

The article on attractiveness and first impressions is Daniel S. Hamermesh, "Ugly? You May Have a Case," *New York Times*, August 28, 2011, www.nytimes.com/2011/08/28/opinion/sunday/ugly-you-may-have-a-case.html.

A common assumption most people make is that physically attractive people are more generally more competent and intelligent than less attractive people. This power of attractiveness is so compelling that people also believe more beautiful people are even better at unrelated tasks, like piloting a plane. Satoshi Kanazawa and Jody L. Kovar, "Why Beautiful People Are More Intelligent," *Intelligence* 32 (2004): 227–43, available at http://mail2.scu.edu.tw/~hltao/Supplement/Ch10/10.3.2AW hy%20beautiful%20people%20are%20more%20intelligent %20%28Kanazawa%202004%20Intelligence%29.pdf.

Catherin Hakim's views on the "beauty premium" are discussed by Celia Walden in "Erotic Capital," *Telegraph* (UK), April 14, 2010, www.telegraph.co.uk/culture/7588813/Erotic-capital.html.

The study measuring the effect of being attractive on those selling drugs to physicians is Michael Ahearne, Thomas W. Gruen, and Cheryl Jarvis, "If Looks Could Sell: Moderation and Mediation of the Attractiveness Effect on Salesperson Performance," *International Journal of Research in Marketing* 16, no. 4 (December 1999): 269–84, http://ssrn.com/abstract=1584809.

While the goal of making a good first impression is easy to understand, implementing it can be confusing for both men and women. Fortunately, a lot of guidance is available on the Internet and in books. Here are some useful resources:

Lahle Wolfe, "Small Business Attire for Women: Dressing for Success," About.com, http://womeninbusiness.about.com/od/businessattireforwomen/a/attirestandards.htm.

Proper Business Attire and Etiquette: Presenting the Complete Package, TCB Solutions.net, http://tcbsolutions.net/Proper_Attire_and_etiquette_for_men_and_women.pdf.

Christopher Muther, "Dress Code—Women's Business Attire," Boston.com, www.boston.com/jobs/topworkplaces/2009/dresstoimpress.

"A Ten-Step GQ Guide to Nailing Office Style," a slideshow on GQ.com, www.gq.com/style/wear-it-now /201110/best-office-style-business-suits-fall.

Jennifer Baumgartner, *You Are What You Wear: What Your Clothes Reveal About You* (Cambridge: Da Capo, 2012). Dr. Baumgartner is a psychologist who brings that expertise to her clothing recommendations.

Editors of Esquire Magazine, *The Handbook of Style: A Man's Guide to Looking Good* (New York: Hearst, 2009).

Chapter 7: Understand the Power of Emotional Connections

For a discussion of what portion of a buying decision is based on emotions, see Diane Berenbaum's article "Four Key Strategies for Building Emotional Connections with Your Customers" on the Communico website, www.communicoltd.com/pages/1076_four_key_strategies_ for_building_emotional_connections_with_your_customers .cfm.

The views of the Gallup Organization on the importance of making emotional connections are set forth by William J. McEwen and John H. Fleming in "Customer Satisfaction Doesn't Count," March 13, 2003, available at www.adobe.com/engagement/pdfs/gmj_customer_satisfaction.pdf.

For a discussion of brain capacity, see the article by Paul Reber (professor of psychology at Northwestern University), "What Is the Memory Capacity of the Human Brain?" on the *Scientific American* website, www.scientificamerican.com/article.cfm?id=what-is-the-memory-capacity. Other estimates of the capacity of the human brain range from one to 1,000 terabytes: "The Technology of Storage," Museum of American Heritage website, www.moah.org/exhibits/archives/brains/technology.html.

You can test your short-term memory for numbers, letters, and words at www.braingle.com/mind/test_numbers.php.

The following paper explores the anomaly between the complexity and processing capacity of our brains and our frustrating inability to retain more than a very limited amount of data in short-term memory: René Marois and Jason Ivanoff, "Capacity Limits of Information Processing in the Brain," *Trends in Cognitive Sciences* 9, no. 6 (June 2005): 296–305, available at www.sciencedirect.com/science/article/pii/S136466130500 1178.

The estimate of the amount of information processed by our brain is set forth by Nick Herbert in *Elemental Mind: Human Consciousness and the New Physics* (New York: Plume, 1994). His findings are discussed in "Working Memory—Where Emotionally and Somatically Tagged Information Gets Prioritized" on the website for J. W. Wilson's book *Cracking the Learning Code*, http://crackingthelearningcode.com/element18.html.

For an explanation of the role emotions play in memory, see "What Role Do Emotions Play in Memory?" on the website *The Human Brain: An Owner's Manual*, created by Eric Heydenberk and Rob Okrzesik, http://library.thinkquest.org/C0114820/emotional/memory. php3.

Another example of the awesome ability of the brain to retain emotional content was provided by neuroscientist Joseph LeDoux: "If you were bitten by your neighbor's dog yesterday, the sight of the beast today (and for some time to come) will certainly put you on guard, causing you, for example, to freeze dead in your tracks, or perhaps to run away, and will also lead to a host of physiological responses." From "Emotion, Memory, and the Brain: What the Lab Does and Why We Do It" on the LeDoux Laboratory website, www.cns.nyu.edu/home/ledoux/overview.html.

For a discussion of how the brain remembers past emotions, see Rebecca M. Todd and Adam K. Anderson, "The Neurogenetics of Remembering Emotions Past," *Proceedings of the National Academy of Sciences* 106, no. 45 (November 10, 2009): 18881–82, available at http://utoronto.academia.edu/RebeccaTodd/Papers/796244/ The_neurogenetics_of_remembering_emotions_past. See also Rebecca M. Todd, Demorah Talmi, Taylor W. Schmitz, Josh Sussking, and Adam K. Anderson, "Psychophysical and Neural Evidence for Emotion-Enhanced Perceptual Vividness," *Journal of Neuroscience* 32, no. 33 (August 15, 2012): 11201–12, doi:10.1523/JNEUROSCI.0155-12.2012, available for purchase at www.jneurosci.org/content/32/33/11201.abstract.

The study on emotions and the memories of those afflicted with Alzheimer's disease is Hiroaki Kazui et al., "Impact of Emotion on Memory: Controlled Study of the Influence of Emotionally Charged Material on Declarative

Memory in Alzheimer's Disease," *British Journal of Psychiatry* 177, no. 4 (October 2000): 343–47, http://bjp.rcpsych.org/content/177/4/343.full.

You can find other examples of emotional data in David Heitman's article "The Emotional Side of Data," *Creative Intelligence Blog*, May 25, 2011, www.thecreativealliance.com/branding/the-emotional-side-of-data.

Dr. Paul MacLean, a respected neuroscientist, reportedly stated, "Something does not exist unless it is tied up with emotions." Quoted in "No Learning Without Emotion" on the website for J. W. Wilson's book *Cracking the Learning Code*, http://crackingthelearningcode.com/element16.html.

Chapter 8: Connect with Your Customers

For a discussion of primary emotions (attributed to the work of psychologist Robert Plutchik), see Virginia Nussey's blog post "The Six-Step Emotional Appeal," *The Raven Blog*, March 16, 2011, http://raventools.com/blog/the-6-step-emotional-appeal.

For a discussion of why customers want an emotional connection, see B. Joseph Pine II and James H. Gilmore,

The Experience Economy, updated ed. (Boston: Harvard Business School Publishing, 2011).

For a discussion of the remarkable lengths to which Zappos will go to make an emotional connection with a customer, see Glenn Rifkin's "Zappos Races Ahead," *Korn/Ferry Briefings on Talent and Leadership*, Spring 2010, www.kornferryinstitute.com/briefings-magazine/spring-2010/zappos-races-ahead.

The role of empathy in making an emotional connection and the way IBM approached its customers are set forth by Dev Patnaik in "Innovation Starts with Empathy," *Design Mind*, September 2009, http://designmind.frogdesign.com/articles/the-substance-of-things-not-seen/innovation-starts-with-empathy.html.

For a discussion of the differences in how men and women view sharing, see Elizabeth Bernstein, "How Much Sharing Is Too Much?," *Wall Street Journal*, July 16, 2009, http://online.wsj.com/article/SB1000142405297020373940 4574286101995111512.html.

For more examples of connecting information with data, see Doug Fleener, "Making the Emotional Sale," Dynamic Experiences Group website,

www.dynamicexperiencesgroup.com/Articles/Making%20t
he%20Emotional%20Sale.pdf.

Chapter 9: Don't Assume

For a discussion of the problems with making assumptions
in sales, see Garry Duncan, "Bad Assumptions Can Doom
Sales Efforts," *Portland Business Journal*, April 15, 2011,
www.bizjournals.com/portland/print-
edition/2011/04/15/bad-assumptions-can-doom-sales-
efforts.html.

The story of the deaf swimmer is told by Susan Lacke
in "Out There: Don't Make Assumptions," *Competitor*,
March 29, 2012,
http://running.competitor.com/2012/03/out-there/out-there-
dont-make-assumptions_50026.

For a host of reasons on why making assumptions is a
bad practice, see Stephanie Ward's article "Why
Assumptions Are Bad For Business," Business Know-How
website,
www.businessknowhow.com/growth/assumptions.htm.

You can find a definition of standard deviation on
Investopedia at

www.investopedia.com/terms/s/standarddeviation.asp#axzz 2GLyIPbyp.

Incorrect assumptions can lead to a number of bad consequences, including stifling growth and development, hindering creativity, and causing missed opportunities, erroneous beliefs, errors in judgment, and misunderstandings. See "The Dangers of Making Assumptions," *Han of Harmony* (blog), November 25, 2010, http://hanofharmony.com/the-dangers-of-making-assumptions.

Chapter 10: Question

Many books have been written on consultative selling. Here are two excellent resources: Mack Hanan, *Consultative Selling: The Hanan Formula for High-Margin Sales at High Levels*, 8th ed. (New York: AMACOM, 2011); and Tim Ursiny and Gary DeMoss with Jim More, *Coaching the Sale: Discover the Power of Coaching to Increase Sales and Build Great Sales Teams* (Naperville, IL: Sourcebooks, 2006). I attended several presentations by Dr. Ursiny at sales conferences and benefited from his insights.

For additional tips on asking sales questions, see Geoffrey James, "Nine Rules for Asking Effective Sales Questions," *Moneywatch* website, September 9, 2010, www.cbsnews.com/8301-505183_162-28551872-10391735/nine-rules-for-asking-effective-sales-questions.

The goals of asking questions are summarized by Erica Stritch in "7 Keys to Leading Highly Effective Sales Conversations," *RainMaker Blog*, www.raintoday.com/blog/7-keys-to-leading-highly-effective-sales-conversations.

For support for "ditching the pitch," see Crystal Collins, "Ditch the Pitch," *Savvy Blogging*, April 4, 2012, http://savvyblogging.net/ditch-the-pitch; and Andrew Sheivachman, "Want Sales? Ditch the Pitch and Ask Questions," *Travel Market Report*, August 16, 2012, www.travelmarketreport.com/articles/Want-Sales-Ditch-the-Pitch-Ask-Questions.

Eric Baron and David Hauer's article discussing consultative selling by pharmaceutical representatives is "Sales Bites: A New Way to Sell Pharmaceuticals," available from the Baron Group at http://barongroup.com/images/Sales_Bites--A_New_Way_to_Sell_Pharmaceuticals.pdf.

Chapter 11: Listen

For helpful tips by Kellie Fowler on developing active listening skills, see the e-booklet *Mind Tools on Active Listening*, www.mindtools.com/CommSkll/Mind%20Tools%20Listening.pdf.

The 80/20 rule is discussed by Claudia Dail, a well-known sales consultant, in "Sales Reps—Are You Applying the 80/20 Rule of Listening?" on her blog *Sell By Caring*, December 16, 2010, www.sellbycaring.com/sales-reps-%E2%80%93-are-you-applying-the-8020-rule-of-listening.

The study in which almost all survey respondents said they were great listeners is cited by W. V. Haney in *Communication and Interpersonal Relations* (Homewood, IL: Irwin, 1979). The study showing how we *really* listen is cited by R. C. Husman, J. M. Lahiff, and J. M. Penrose in *Business Communication: Strategies and Skills* (Chicago: Dryden Press, 1988). Both studies are referenced by Dr. Scott Williams in "Listening Effectively," Wright State University website, www.wright.edu/~scott.williams/skills/listening.htm.

Curiously, most people believe they have no need to improve their own listening skills.

You can find many examples of productive questions to ask prospects in "Top 30 Open-Ended Questions," *Just Sell* (blog), www.justsell.com/top-30-open-ended-questions (sign-in required to read full article).

For more information about how detectives are trained to listen, see Mike Brooks, "How to Listen Like a Detective," Evan Carmichael website, www.evancarmichael.com/Sales/3114/How-to-Listen-like-a-Detective.html.

The experience of Dr. Scott Williams is described in his article "Listening Effectively," Wright State University website, www.wright.edu/~scott.williams/skills/listening.htm.

For a discussion on the issue of women being interrupted more frequently than men, see Ellen Spertus, "Ways that Males and Females Are Treated Differently," in *Why Are There So Few Female Computer Scientists?* (MIT Artificial Intelligence Laboratory Technical Report 1315, 1991), http://people.mills.edu/spertus/Gender/pap/node7.html. Also see Charlotte A. Morris, "The Effects of Gender on

Communication in the Legal Profession," North Carolina Bar Association website, June 16, 2009, http://wip.ncbar.org/media/2754960/effectsofgenderoncommunication.pdf.

Chapter 12: Connect with Both Men and Women

For a discussion of the social bonding and stress-reducing effects of oxytocin, see "Oxytocin—the Elixir of Trust" on the Brainsex Matters website, http://brainsexmatters.com/news.php.

For a discussion of the different impacts oxytocin may have on men and women, see Lauren A. McCarthy, "Evolutionary and Biochemical Explanations for a Unique Female Stress Response: Tend-and-Befriend," on the Great Ideas in Personality website at www.personalityresearch.org/papers/mccarthy.html.

For a discussion of the effect of vasopressin on aggression, see C. F. Ferris, "Vasopressin/Oxytocin and Aggression," in *Molecular Mechanisms Influencing Aggressive Behaviours: Novartis Foundation Symposium 268*, ed. G. Bock and J. Goode (Chichester, UK: Wiley,

2008), doi:10.1002/0470010703.ch13, abstract available at www.ncbi.nlm.nih.gov/pubmed/16206881.

The study on the differences in how men and women communicate is described by Jennifer Coates in *Women, Men and Language: A Sociolinguistic Account of Gender Differences*, 3rd ed. (Pearson Longman, 2004).

For a discussion of how men and women have difficulty communicating, see Deborah Tannen, *You Just Don't Understand: Women and Men in Conversation* (New York: William Morrow, 1990). Other research shows that men speak more loudly than women, are less inquisitive, and are more accusatory, as discussed by Lillian Glass in *He Says, She Says: Closing the Communication Gap Between the Sexes* (New York: Perigee, 1995). Ms. Glass also notes differences in body language and facial expressions. She found that women engage in close eye contact more often than men, and that men tend to lean back, whereas women lean forward.

You can find useful tips for selling to women in Mary Clare Hunt's *In Women We Trust: A Cultural Shift to the Softer Side of Business* (WME Books, 2006) and in her article based on the research in her book, "Do's and Don'ts for Selling to Women Small Business Owners," Small Business Trends website, September 5, 2006,

· http://smallbiztrends.com/2006/09/dos-and-donts-for-selling-to-women-small-business-owners.html. In addition to other suggestions, Hunt recommends against having a set goal or agenda and making patronizing comments (such as a man saying, "I like women—my wife is a woman.").

For a discussion about how gender differences are not "hardwired," see Lise Eliot, "Girl Brain, Boy Brain?," *Scientific American*, September 8, 2009, www.scientificamerican.com/article.cfm?id=girl-brain-boy-brain.

The awesome buying power of women is discussed by Cynthia Tidwell in "Selling to Women: Ditch the Pitch," *Life Insurance Selling*, April 1, 2010, reprinted on the *LifeHealthPro* website at www.lifehealthpro.com/2010/04/01/selling-to-women-ditch-the-pitch.

The buying power of women and their influence on purchases should not be underestimated. Women control over $20 trillion in worldwide spending, purchase more than half of all new cars bought in the US, and spend over $200 billion on new cars and vehicle servicing each year. Yet 75 percent of women surveyed feel misunderstood by car marketers, 84 percent feel misunderstood by investment marketers, and a whopping 91 percent of women in one survey said that advertisers don't understand them. These people have not learned how to sell to women. "Fast Facts," on the website of the ninth annual Marketing to Women conference, www.m2w.biz/fast_facts.php.

Chapter 13: Limit Use of PowerPoint

For an excellent article on the impact of visuals in PowerPoint and other settings, see Mike Parkinson, "The Power of Visual Communication," Mike Parkinson's Billion Dollar Graphics website, www.billiondollargraphics.com/infographics.html.

As a guide for my tips on creating effective PowerPoint designs in large group settings, I used information from Joshua Johnson, "10 Tips for Designing Presentations That Don't Suck: Pt. 1," *Design Shack* (blog), September 3, 2010, http://designshack.net/articles/graphics/10-tips-for-designing-presentations-that-dont-suck-pt-1.

Chapter 14: E-Connect

For a discussion of the size of the e-commerce market, see Allison Enright, "E-commerce Sales Jump 16% in 2011," *Internet Retailer*, February 16, 2012, www.internetretailer.com/2012/02/16/e-commerce-sales-jump-16-2011.

For projections of increasing e-commerce sales, see Shea Bennett, "Social Media, Mobile and the Rapid Growth of E-commerce," Mediabistro's AllTwitter website, September 5, 2012, www.mediabistro.com/alltwitter/e-commerce-social-mobile_b27953.

The factors establishing trustworthiness in a website are discussed in a report by Cheskin Research and Studio Archetype/Sapient, *eCommerce Trust Study*, January 1999, www.added-value.com/source/wp-content/uploads/2012/01/17__report-eComm-Trust1999.pdf.

For a link to the Google video promoting Google+, together with a discussion of the powerful emotional connection made by this video, see David Hartstein's blog post "Using Emotion to Connect with Website Visitors," *WiredImpact* blog, May 23, 2012, http://wiredimpact.com/blog/using-emotion-with-website-visitors. Additional examples of viral videos that succeeded in making an emotional connection are discussed in "Top 5 Branded Viral Videos of the Week Ending June 2, 2012," ViralGains website, June 2, 2012, http://blog.viralgains.com/2012/06/top-5-branded-viral-videos-of-the-week-ending-june-2-2012.

The quote attributed to Milton Pedraza appears in Molly Selvin's article "Perfume Gifts Smelling Good to Shoppers," *Los Angeles Times*, December 17, 2007, http://articles.latimes.com/2007/dec/17/business/fi-perfume. Few people realize that the formulation of Chanel No. 5 remains unique, consisting of expensive ingredients that had never been formulated in this way before. For a discussion of the ingredients of Chanel No. 5, see Barbara Herman, "Chanel No. 5 (1921)," *Yesterday's Perfume* (blog), June 29, 2010, http://yesterdaysperfume.typepad.com/yesterdays_perfume/2010/06/chanel-no-5-1921.html. For whatever reason, no one can quarrel with the remarkable success of this perfume. By some estimates a bottle of Chanel No. 5 is sold every fifty-five seconds all over the world.

You can find Marilyn Monroe's advertising copy at "The Real Thing—Chanel No. 5," *Luxury Studies* (blog), April 30, 2011, http://luxurystudies.blogspot.com/2011/04/real-thing-chanel-no-5.html.

A study on the effectiveness of banner ads that connect to emotions is reported by Hamish Pringle and Peter Field in *Brand Immortality: How Brands Can Live Long and Prosper* (London: Kogan Page, 2009). It is also discussed by Roger Dooley in "Emotional Ads Work Best," *Neuromarketing* (blog), July 27, 2009, www.neurosciencemarketing.com/blog/articles/emotional-ads-work-best.htm. Another study looked at the impact of emotional content in banner ads and reached the same conclusion: "Frank" Tian Xie, Naveen Donthu, Ritu Lohtia, and Talai Osmonbekov, "Emotional Appeal and Incentive Offering in Banner Advertisements," *Journal of Interactive Advertising* 4, no. 2 (Spring 2004): 43–54, http://faculty.lebow.drexel.edu/SuriR/Marketing%20Facult y%20Journal%20%20Pdf%20Files/emotional%20appeal% 20and%20incentive%20offering.pdf.

Chapter 15: The Happiness-Success Relationship

Data on the effect of winning the lottery on happiness can be found in "Lottery Winner Statistics," Statistic Brain website, www.statisticbrain.com/lottery-winner-statistics.

For a discussion of extrinsic and intrinsic goals, see Tim Kasser and Richard M. Ryan, "Further Examining the American Dream: Differential Correlates of Intrinsic and

Extrinsic Goals," *Personality and Social Psychology Bulletin* 22, no. 3 (March 1996): 280–87,

> http://psp.sagepub.com/content/22/3/280.abstract.

The article questioning whether high income is related to happiness is Daniel Kahneman, Alan B. Krueger, David Schkade, Norbert Schwarz, and Arthur A. Stone, "Would You Be Happier If You Were Richer? A Focusing Illusion," *Science* 312, no. 5782 (June 30, 2006): 1908–10, available at

www.princeton.edu/~ceps/workingpapers/125krueger.pdf.

The article by Jennifer Aaker that summarizes research relating happiness to various factors is "Designing Happiness: Insights from Readings," available on the Stanford University website, http://faculty-gsb.stanford.edu/aaker/pages/documents/AllReadingInsights2.pdf.

The study on the amount of income necessary to reach a base level of happiness is Daniel Kahneman and Angus Deaton, "High Income Improves Evaluation of Life but Not Emotional Well-Being," *Proceedings of the National Academy of Sciences* 107, no. 38 (September 21, 2010): 16489–93, available at

www.pnas.org/content/107/38/16489.abstract. While daily happiness plateaus at the $75,000 household income threshold, those who earned more money had higher levels of overall satisfaction with their lives.

Another study measuring the happiness of 909 women who resided in Texas found that watching television, sex, socializing, and relaxing made them happy: D. Kahneman, A. B. Krueger, D. A. Schkade, N. Schwartz, and A. A. Stone, "A Survey Method for Characterizing Daily Life Experience: The Day Reconstruction Method," *Science* 306, no. 5702 (December 3, 2004): 1776–80. This study is discussed by Benedict Carey in "What Makes People Happy? TV, Study Says," *New York Times*, December 2, 2004,

www.nytimes.com/2004/12/02/health/02cnd-mood.html.

The study demonstrating the relationship between happiness and success is Sonja Lyubomirsky, Laura King, and Ed Diener, "The Benefits of Frequent Positive Affect: Does Happiness Lead to Success?" *Psychological Bulletin* 131, no. 6 (November 2005): 803–55,

www.faculty.ucr.edu/~sonja/papers/LKD2005.pdf. The study is discussed in "Review of Research Challenges Assumption That Success Makes People Happy," *ScienceDaily*, December 19, 2005,

www.sciencedaily.com/releases/2005/12/051219090811.ht m. The underlying survey is Tom W. Smith, "Job Satisfaction in the United States,"
www-news.uchicago.edu/releases/07/pdf/070417.jobs.pdf.

Chapter 16: The Sad State of Happiness

The study of levels of happiness in various countries was reported by Peter Whoriskey in "If You're Happy and You Know It...Let the Government Know," *Washington Post*, March 29, 2012,
www.washingtonpost.com/business/economy/if-youre-happy-and-you-know-it-let-the-government-know/2012/03/29/gIQAlSL2jS_story.html.

The survey finding a majority of Americans unhappy at work was reported by Bill Ritter in "60 Percent of Americans Are Unhappy at Work," May 30, 2012, available on the website of WABC-TV,
http://abclocal.go.com/wabc/story?section=news/lifestyle& id=8681276.

The happiness study from Pew Research is *Are We Happy Yet?* Pew Research Center, February 13, 2006, http://pewresearch.org/assets/social/pdf/AreWeHappyYet.p df.

Studies on the average level of happiness of men and women over time and as they age are discussed by Marcus Buckingham in "What's Happening to Women's Happiness?," *Huffington Post*, September 17, 2009, www.huffingtonpost.com/marcus-buckingham/whats-happening-to-womens_b_289511.html.

Suggestions for how to be unhappy are from Celestine Chua, "How to Be Unhappy: 10 Surefire Ways to Be Unhappy in Life," *Personal Excellence* (blog), http://personalexcellence.co/blog/how-to-be-unhappy.

You can find Deepak Chopra's explanation for why so many people seem committed to a life of unhappiness in his article "Why You Don't Want to Be Happy" on the Beliefnet website, http://blog.beliefnet.com/intentchopra/2010/11/why-you-dont-want-to-be-happy.html.

Chapter 17: Eliminate the Source of Unhappiness

For a helpful discussion of the different types of therapies available, see the article "Psychotherapies" on the National Institute of Mental Health website, www.nimh.nih.gov/health/topics/psychotherapies/index.sht ml.

The extensive research supporting the use of cognitive behavioral therapy is discussed and cited by David Pollak in "Why Psychologists Love Using Cognitive Behavior Therapy (CBT) for Depression," *SelfhelpMagazine*, July 5, 2012, www.selfhelpmagazine.com/articles/CBT.

The *Time* magazine article discussing the benefits of cognitive therapy is by Lev Grossman, "Talk Therapy: Can Freud Get His Job Back?," *Time*, January 20, 2003, www.time.com/time/magazine/article/0,9171,1004088,00.h tml.

For information about clinical trials sponsored by the National Institute of Mental Health, see "Clinical Trials" on the NIMH website, www.nimh.nih.gov/trials/index.shtml. For information about low-cost cognitive behavioral providers, see "Low Cost Cognitive Therapist," Academy of Cognitive Therapy website, www.academyofct.org/i4a/pages/index.cfm?pageid=3449.

The job happiness survey was conducted from 1986 to 2006 by the General Social Survey at the National Opinion Research Center at the University of Chicago. The results are reported in this news release: "Looking for satisfaction and happiness in a career? Start by choosing a job that

helps others," University of Chicago News Office, April 17, 2007,
www-news.uchicago.edu/releases/07/070417.jobs.shtml.

For a psychologist's assessment of the significance of the ten happiest and ten most hated jobs, see Deborah Khoshaba, "Do You Need Money and Status to Be Happy on the Job?," *Get Hardy* blog on the *Psychology Today* website, December 9, 2011,
www.psychologytoday.com/blog/get-hardy/201112/do-you-need-money-and-status-be-happy-the-job.

For suggestions on making your job work better for you, see Susan M. Heathfield's article "How to Make Your Current Job Work," About.com,
http://humanresources.about.com/od/careerplanningandadvice1/a/time_to_go.htm. For a discussion of reasons to quit your job, see Heathfield's article "Top 10 Reasons to Quit Your Job," About.com,
http://humanresources.about.com/od/whenemploymentends/a/quit_job.htm.

Chapter 18: Make Positive Changes to Increase Happiness

The amount of happiness we can control is discussed by Sonja Lyubomirsky in "What Influences Our Happiness the Most?," *How of Happiness* blog on the *Psychology Today* website, May 4, 2008, www.psychologytoday.com/blog/how-happiness/200805/what-influences-our-happiness-the-most.

Shawn Achor discusses the findings he set forth in his book *The Happiness Advantage* (New York: Crown Business, 2010) in "Is Happiness the Secret of Success?" CNN website, March 19, 2012, www.cnn.com/2012/03/19/opinion/happiness-success-achor/index.html.

Studies on the effect of making an emotional connection on happiness are discussed in "Connection and Happiness," an article on the website for the PBS series *This Emotional Life*, www.pbs.org/thisemotionallife/topic/connecting/connectio n-happiness.

The myriad benefits of empathy are discussed by Elizabeth DeVita-Raeburn in "Empathy: How It Changes Your Friendships, Job and Life," *Self*, December 2011, www.self.com/health/2011/12/how-empathy-changes-friendships-jobs-life.

The many benefits of reflective listening are discussed by Neil Katz and Kevin McNulty in "Reflective Listening," which can be downloaded from the website of the Maxwell School of Syracuse University, Program for the Advancement of Research on Conflict and Collaboration, www.maxwell.syr.edu/uploadedFiles/parcc/cmc/Reflective%20Listening%20NK.pdf.

Dalmar Fisher's *Communication in Organizations*, 2nd ed. (Mumbai, India: Jaico, 2006) provides an excellent discussion and examples of reflective listening. Material drawn from Fisher's book can be found at "Active Listening," Analytic Technologies website, www.analytictech.com/mb119/reflecti.htm.

Studies discussing the effect of sharing money or treats with others are reported by Elizabeth Dunn and Michael Norton in "Don't Indulge. Be Happy," *New York Times*, July 8, 2012, www.nytimes.com/2012/07/08/opinion/sunday/dont-indulge-be-happy.html.

The study on the benefits of volunteering is discussed in "Altruism and Happiness" on the website for the PBS series *This Emotional Life*, www.pbs.org/thisemotionallife/topic/altruism/altruism-happiness.

The *Christian Science Monitor* article referencing five hundred studies on the relationship between generosity and happiness is by Jane Lampman, "Researchers Say Giving Leads to a Healthier, Happier Life," July 25, 2007, www.csmonitor.com/2007/0725/p13s02-lire.html. The same article cites the study that showed how the brain responds to thinking about engaging in a charitable act.

For a discussion of how the Internet is providing opportunities for altruism, see Dana Klisanin, "Is the Internet Giving Rise to New Forms of Altruism?," *Media Psychology Review* (online), http://mprcenter.org/mpr/index.php?option=com_content&view=article&id=215&Itemid=180.

You can learn more about Taylor Marie Crabtree and read additional stories about acts of kindness on the web page "Random Acts of Kindness Edition...33 Heartfelt 'Stories of Kindness,'" *A Magazine of People and Possibilities*, www.peopleandpossibilities.com/33kindnessstories2.html.

The study showing the effects of acts of kindness performed by children is Kristin Layous, S. Katherine Nelson, Eva Oberle, Kimberly A. Schonert-Reichi, and

Sonja Lyubomirsky, "Kindness Counts: Prompting Prosocial Behavior in Preadolescents Boosts Peer Acceptance and Well-Being," *PLoS ONE* 7, no. 12 (December 2012), www.plosone.org/article/info%3Adoi%2F10.1371%2Fjournal.pone.0051380.

Gretchen Rubin notes that feelings of happiness from doing random acts of kindness may be based on a faulty assumption: you believe you will be making the recipient of your conduct happy. In fact, many people react to acts of kindness with suspicion. See her article "Happiness Myth No. 7: Doing 'Random Acts of Kindness' Brings Happiness," *The Happiness Project* (blog), March 10, 2009, www.happinessproject.com/happiness_project/2009/03/happiness-myth-no-7-doing-random-acts-of-kindness-brings-happiness.

Other studies demonstrate that subjective happiness was increased just by counting acts of kindness for one week: Keiko Otake, Satoshi Shimai, Junko Tanaka-Matsumi, Kanako Otsui, and Barbara L. Fredrickson, "Happy People Become Happier Through Kindness: A Counting Kindnesses Intervention," *Journal of Happiness Studies* 7, no. 3 (September 2006): 361–75, available at www.ncbi.nlm.nih.gov/pmc/articles/PMC1820947.

For a study demonstrating that pleasurable experiences are a greater source of happiness than material purchases, see Leaf Van Boven and Thomas Gilovich, "To Do or to Have? That Is the Question," *Journal of Personality and Social Psychology* 85, no. 6 (December 2003): 1193–1202, http://bit.ly/W8r537.

The blog post listing hundreds of positive experiences is by Rob Kall, "The K.P.E.I., Kall Positive Experience Inventory," *Positive Experience*, www.positiveexperience.com/populum/page.php?f=THE-K-P-E-I-KALL-POSITIVE-by-Rob-Kall-090627-884.html.

The study measuring the effect of playfulness in adults is René T. Proyer, "Examining Playfulness in Adults: Testing Its Correlates with Personality, Positive Psychological Functioning, Goal Aspirations, and Multi-methodically Assessed Ingenuity," *Psychological Test and Assessment Modeling* 54, no. 2 (2012), 103–27, www.psychologieaktuell.com/fileadmin/download/ptam/2-2012_20120628/01_proyer.pdf.

The impact of diet and exercise on overall health is discussed in this paper: US Department of Health and Human Services, *Physical Activity Fundamental to Preventing Disease*, July 20, 2002, http://aspe.hhs.gov/health/reports/physicalactivity.

The relationship between diet and cancer is discussed in "Make Over Your Diet: How Does My Diet Affect My Health?," NutritionMD,

www.nutritionmd.org/makeover/index.html.

Chapter 19: Meditate

The book that started me on my meditation journey is Jon Kabat-Zinn, *Full Catastrophe Living: Using the Wisdom of Your Body and Mind to Face Stress, Pain, and Illness,* reprinted. (New York: Delta, 1990). You can order the audio CDs from Kabat-Zinn's website "Mindfulness Meditation Practice CDs and Tapes,"

www.mindfulnesscds.com/series1.html.

I have no affiliation with the author.

Here are some other meditation resources you may find helpful:

Susan Piver, ed., *Quiet Mind: A Beginner's Guide to Meditation* (Boston: Shambhala, 2008). Book with accompanying CD of guided instructions.

Jon Kabat-Zinn, *Mindfulness for Beginners: Reclaiming the Present Moment—and Your Life* (Boulder, CO: Sounds True, 2012).

Marc Allen, *How to Quiet Your Mind: Relax and Silence the Voice of Your Mind, Today!* (Empowerment Nation, 2011).

I obtained information about the scope of research on transcendental meditation from "The Technique," Transcendental Meditation Program website, www.tm.org/meditation-techniques.

The study showing the effects of meditation on the brain circuits responsible for empathy and other emotions is A. Lutz, J. Brefczynski-Lewis, T. Johnstone, and R. J. Davidson, "Regulation of the Neural Circuitry of Emotion by Compassion Meditation: Effects of Meditative Expertise," *PLoS ONE* 3, no. 3 (March 2008): e1897, doi:10.1371/journal.pone.0001897, www.plosone.org/article/fetchArticle.action?articleURI=info:doi/10.1371/journal.pone.0001897. Another study reaching the same result is discussed by Lindsay Abrams in "Study: Meditation Can Make Us More Empathetic," *Atlantic*, October 7, 2012, www.theatlantic.com/health/archive/2012/10/study-meditation-can-make-us-more-empathetic/263307.

A study showing the different responses to sounds of suffering by those who meditated and those who didn't is

A. Lutz et al., "Regulation of the Neural Circuitry," cited above.

The views of the Mayo Clinic on the benefits of meditation can be found in "Meditation: A Simple, Fast Way to Reduce Stress," Mayo Clinic website, www.mayoclinic.com/health/meditation/HQ01070.

The study on the effects of transcendental meditation on blood pressure is J. W. Anderson, C. Lui, and R. J. Kryscio, "Blood Pressure Response to Transcendental Meditation: A Meta-analysis," *American Journal of Hypertension* 21, no. 3 (March 2008): 310–16, www.ncbi.nlm.nih.gov/pubmed/18311126. The authors of the study concluded that "the regular practice of Transcendental Meditation may have the potential to reduce systolic and diastolic blood pressure by approximately 4.7 and 3.2 mm Hg, respectively. These are clinically meaningful changes."

The study on the effect of meditation on high-risk cardiovascular participants is Robert Schneider et al., "Effects of Stress Reduction on Clinical Events in African Americans with Coronary Heart Disease: A Randomized Controlled Trial," *Circulation* 120, S461 (2009), http://circ.ahajournals.org/cgi/content/meeting_abstract/120/18_MeetingAbstracts/S461-a.

The study showing an increase in the area of the brain responsible for learning and memory after eight weeks of meditation is Britta K. Hölzel et al., "Mindfulness Practice Leads to Increases in Regional Brain Gray Matter Density," *Psychiatry Research: Neuroimaging* 191, no. 1 (January 30, 2011): 36–43, www.psyn-journal.com/article/S0925-4927%2810%2900288-X/ abstract.

The UCLA study on the brain differences in long-term meditators is discussed in a UCLA news release by Mark Wheeler, "Evidence Builds that Meditation Strengthens the Brain, UCLA Researchers Say," March 14, 2012, http://newsroom.ucla.edu/portal/ucla/evidence-builds-that-meditation-230237.aspx.

The study showing the impact of different kinds of meditation techniques on divergent and convergent thinking is Lorenza S. Colzato, Ayca Ozturk, and Bernhard Hommel, "Meditate to Create: The Impact of Focused-Attention and Open-Monitoring Training on Convergent and Divergent Thinking," *Frontiers in Psychology*, April 18, 2012, doi:10.3389/fpsyg.2012.00116, www.frontiersin.org/Cognition/10.3389/fpsyg.2012.00116/ abstract.

The study showing how meditation affects pain is reported in "Demystifying Meditation: Brain Imaging

Illustrates How Meditation Reduces Pain," *ScienceDaily*, April 11, 2011, www.sciencedaily.com/releases/2011/04/110405174835.htm.

The study showing a shift from stress-prone to calmer areas of the brain is discussed by Colin Allen in "The Benefits of Meditation," *Psychology Today*, April 1, 2003, www.psychologytoday.com/articles/200304/the-benefits-meditation.

Chapter 20: Make It Happen

The study on increasing fruit consumption is Christopher J. Armitage, "Effects of an Implementation Intention-Based Intervention on Fruit Consumption," *Psychology Health* 22, no. 8 (September 28, 2007): 917–28, www.mendeley.com/research/effects-implementation-intention-based-intervention-fruit-consumption.

Studies referring to success in attaining a number of different kinds of goals are referenced by Amy N. Dalton and Stephen A. Spiller in "Too Much of a Good Thing: The Benefits of Implementation Intentions Depend on the Number of Goals," *Journal of Consumer Research* 39, no. 3 (October 2012): 600–614, www.bm.ust.hk/mark/staff/Amy/Amy-JCR-2012.pdf.

Guidelines based on the Dartmouth College study about goal setting are presented in "The Goal Setting Process" on the website of the Office of Human Resources, Dartmouth College, www.dartmouth.edu/~hrs/profldev/performance_managem ent/goal_setting_process.html.

The studies about the effect of optimism and goal achievement are discussed by Suzanne C. Segerstrom and Lise Solberg Nes in "When Goals Conflict But People Prosper: The Case of Dispositional Optimism," *Journal of Research in Personality* 40, no. 5 (October 2006): 675–93, www.ncbi.nlm.nih.gov/pmc/articles/PMC1578496.

The many positive benefits of optimism are set forth by Suzanne C. Segerstrom in "Optimistic Expectancies and Immunity: Context Matters," *European Health Psychologist* 12, no. 3 (September 2010): 36–38, www.ehps.net/ehp/issues/2010/v12iss3_September2010/12 _3_segerstrom.pdf; and by Charles S. Carver, Michael F. Scheir, and Suzanne C. Segerstrom in "Optimism," *Clinical Psychology Review* 30 (2010): 879–89, www.psy.miami.edu/faculty/ccarver/documents/10_CPR_ Optimism.pdf.

For helpful suggestions on how to turn pessimism into optimism, see "Kill Your Pessimism, Change Your Life,"

TheHappySelf.com, www.thehappyself.com/kill-your-pessimism-change-your-life, and Ebbi Thomas, "Pessimist to Optimist: How to Change Your Viewpoint," Effective Mind Control, www.effective-mind-control.com/pessimist-to-optimist.html.

Psychologist and clinical researcher Martin E. P. Seligman discusses the negative effects of pessimism and ways to change from pessimism to optimism in his book *Learned Optimism* (New York: Knopf, 1991). Psychiatrist David D. Burns discusses the distorted views of pessimists and drug-free cures in his book *Feeling Good: The New Mood Therapy*, rev. ed. (New York: HarperCollins, 1999).

For estimates of the prevalence of narcissistic personality disorder, see Dr. Sam Vaknin, "Narcissistic Personality Disorder—Prevalence and Comorbidity," http://samvak.tripod.com/personalitydisorders13.html. Regardless of the accuracy of this estimate, it appears to be the view of many psychologists that narcissism is on the rise. See Sadie F. Dingfelder, "Reflecting on Narcissism," *Monitor on Psychology* 42, no. 2 (February 2011): 64, www.apa.org/monitor/2011/02/narcissism.aspx.

See the American Psychiatric Association's description of the traits of a narcissist in *Diagnostic and Statistical*

Manual of Mental Disorders, 4th ed. (American Psychiatric Assn., 1994).

Marshall Goldsmith sets forth his views on change in "What Behavior Do You Want to Change?" *BloombergBusinessWeek*, May 6, 2008, www.businessweek.com/stories/2008-05-06/what-behavior-do-you-want-to-change-businessweek-business-news-stock-market-and-financial-advice.

Goldsmith attributes the exercise of asking participants to complete a sentence indicating what traits they would like to improve to another psychologist, Nathaniel Branden.

INDEX